Damaged Soul

One American Story

BY *Mary R. Arnold*

BASED ON A TRUE STORY

Mary Arnold Books
P.O. Box 814
Chesterfield, SC 29709

Cover design by Mary Arnold

ISBN: 978-0-9886373-0-6

Library of Congress Control Number: 2012922177

While this composition is based on a true story, names have been changed to protect the innocent.

Printed in the United States of America

Dedication

To my children and grandchildren:

Teyon, Leyon, D'nita, Makeida, and Jaden

Acknowledgments

This book reports of several events which were hurtful to the author. While it was extremely therapeutic and, therefore, beneficial, it was also extremely difficult to relive those events. This author called upon God's assistance on many different occasions during the year it took to provide this body of work. I thank you Father for always being there for me and, most of all, for providing your only Son – that I might be saved.

Many thanks to the numerous angels God placed in my path to help me find my way through a great turbulence, including: Alice and Walter Cooper, Naomi Jackson, Jasper Howard, Annie Mae and Wardell Jackson, Jr., Maxwell Jackson, Jr., Ivory Moore, III, Beverly Ray, Marcellus Arnold, Carolyn Hudgins, Theresa Butler and Freeman Isaac. Your assistance has been absolutely invaluable.

Table of Contents

Father,

I pray that through the words contained amongst these pages You will grant knowledge, wisdom and Your heavenly favor. In the name of Jesus Christ, Amen.

Preface

"Life Marks" are the significant events of an individual's existence; those events which help to define an individual's character. This book is the accumulation of events that form a story – one American story.

Amongst the pages of this book can be found an account of significant Life Marks of one particular person. One never knows what another person may have experienced or might be experiencing; be patient with others.

There are advantages to being born poor; not many, of course, but some very important advantages. When the eyes are not clouded by money or the things that money can buy, the range of visibility can more easily include things such as honesty and integrity.

Can you imagine witnessing the murder of your eight month old baby sister when you were but a toddler? How would your life have developed? Would the tender psyche of your young mind have remained intact or would you be providing the means by which a well educated, impersonal psychiatrist could afford a beautiful suburban home with perfect landscaping?

In America, we expect every child to have a blissful existence. For the most part, American childhoods are well within our circle of dreams. Yet, for a large number of children, small percentage though it may be, hell is experienced at tender ages; ages at which we are ill-equipped to cope. Ask yourself, if pedophilia is so rampant within our nation, how many children have visited hell; if drug abuse, alcoholism, missing children, gangs, abusive foster care . . . how many?

For the record, it provides no solace to know that there are others who may be just as, or more damaged.

God made each of us from a different mold, so you may not be able to judge how you might have fared given this set of circumstances. Yet and still, you may wish to make comparisons, if only to count your blessings.

Introduction

How horrible when a loved one passes away on or around a holiday. For all eternity that holiday will never again be as happy an occasion as when you were able to share it with your loved one. Instead, it will forever mark the timing of your loss.

Sunday, November 26, 2000. The prior Thursday was Thanksgiving.

ℝ · | · ℞

Mary knew her mother was sick, seriously ill. Her bedroom door was located across the hallway and slightly adjacent to Mary's bedroom. Approximately six weeks prior to her death, Mary stepped into the hallway from her bedroom and saw her mother heading down the hallway toward the bedrooms when she lost her balance, as though she was about to faint. Mary quickly stepped forward to catch her. She asked, "Ma, are you alright?"

She actually giggled and said, "Yeah baby, I'm alright."

Mary tried to get her to see a doctor or visit an emergency room. No go. She once told her children that she had a bad medical experience as a young fifteen year old teenager at a hospital in South Carolina. She never told of the incident itself or even of the medical procedure; but surely it was the reason for her grave apprehension of all things related to the medical community.

Over the next couple of weeks Mary watched her mother grow weaker by the day. Finally, she telephoned her brother and sister. She informed them of their mother's illness, the fact that she could not get her to seek medical attention, and warned that they should come to visit with her soon because there may not be many more such opportunities.

Quickly, the word spread throughout the extended family and Mary's mom was barraged with pleas to see a doctor. Most often her replies were short quips meant to discourage the plea: "No thank you," "Leave me alone," or "Mind your own business."

As Mary and her sons attempted to nurse her mother back to health, Mary also tried to prepare herself for the inevitable. It was an impossible task. She could not predict the void caused by the loss of her mother until it slapped her in the face. As selfish as it sounds, Mary's greatest pain was to be found in the loss of the opportunity to strengthen their mother/daughter relationship.

That is not to say that she did not try when there was still a chance or even that there was no progress made in that regard; it is to say, however, that Mary was not satisfied with the results of those prior efforts. The prevalent question was, *What could I have done differently to make our relationship better?*

Needless to say she did a lot of soul searching in the void created by her mother's absence. Suddenly there were memories flooding back to her from a black hole within her mind. There were painful memories; many of which are laid forth in the following pages.

Pre-Existence

From a higher plane of existence than experienced here on earth there was a gathering of souls. There seemed to be more of an understanding amongst those present than any actual communication.

A soul was about to depart for its adventure on the planet earth. There was excitement in the air. Just as the soul was about to make its departure, an additional soul joined the group. There was a plea not to go.

Both the departing and pleading souls recognized one another as soul mates. With sadness and regret, the departing soul communicated the helplessness of the situation. A woman had prayed desperately and tearfully for someone to love her.

"I must go; now."

Life Mark: Incompetence

It was Easter Sunday, April 13, 1952, in the small town of Cheraw, South Carolina; located approximately thirty miles south of the North Carolina state line and approximately one hundred miles inland of Myrtle Beach, South Carolina.

Unbeknownst to her, she was born into the light; the firstborn to teenage parents. Her mother was sixteen years old, the youngest of eight children; her nineteen year old father was the youngest of seven children.

On the very day of her birth she fell under the attack of evil, in the form of incompetence. Evil has no specific name, race or form. Evil cares not about the people it attacks or those it uses to perform the attacks. It simply appears, attacks then departs; no doubt hoping that it has wrought destruction with its latest attack. Evil can appear in the form of family, friends, and most egregiously, in the form of professionals – professionals for whose services one has paid dearly. *Yet, evil, get back! You shall not win!*

In 1952, doctors still made house calls. She was born at home and shared her birthday with the doctor who performed the delivery.

The doctor addressed Etta and Isaiah, Jr., "Your child's got herself an extra long tongue. I need to clip the end of her tongue."

"Why can't it stay the way it is?" The alarm was audibly evident in Etta's voice.

"It won't do her any good like that and might cause her to choke while she's sleeping."

"Can you do it here? I don't want her to go to the hospital." Isaiah clearly did not want to part with his daughter. "If you can do what you have to do right here, then do it."

"Yeah, I can take care of it with what's in my doctor's bag."

Etta and Isaiah exchanged looks, concern visible on both their faces. They were reluctant to have this procedure performed on their baby, but neither wanted to lose their child in her sleep because they had not heeded the warning of a medical expert.

They watched as the doctor poured alcohol over the sharp blade of a scalpel.

Etta asked with a shaky voice, "Is this going to hurt her?"

"It will, but because she's just born it will just be for a quick minute. Plus, she's too young for pain medicine."

Then he cut the end of the child's tongue, and seemingly oblivious to her cries, he handed her back to Etta while holding gauze over the fresh cut. "Hold that on there for a little bit and it will stop bleeding."

As a result of the tongue-clipping she possesses a condition which the dental community refers to as a tongue thrust. She pushes her tongue against her front teeth (instead of the roof of her mouth) when she swallows, resulting in front teeth that flared outward.

The problem would later be corrected; or rather, it would be dealt with, but not without countless visits to too many dental specialists, not to mention the money spent – money which was unavailable.

To further mark her birth, the parents disagreed about what to name their daughter. Isaiah thought it was special that his first child was born on Easter and wanted to name her Easter Serena. Etta would not hear of it. She chose the name of one sister from either side of the family, Mary, one of Isaiah's sisters, and Ruth, one of her sisters. Isaiah acquiesced, but wanted to provide some sort of protest so, when Etta presented him with the completed record of the child's birth, to be filed at the courthouse, Isaiah decided there was no need to file it. Mary Ruth has no birth certificate.

ℒℴ · | · ℛℯ

It bears mention here, as this story slips back and forth between timeframes, that the parents later separated, shortly following the birth of their second child, a boy, Isaiah III, and while both children could still be categorized as toddlers.

As the story goes, Etta left her home in South Carolina alone. She went to Washington, DC to secure a place in the home of one of her siblings who lived there, then returned to South Carolina to "snatch" her children while her husband was not looking. Etta was heard to say, "These are *my* children!" Etta, who was already known to be very protective of her children, had actually moved beyond protective or even over-protective, to possessive.

Mary should have realized that there was violence in her parent's marriage. She may even have witnessed some of it, but was too young to have registered any such memories. In fact, she had no memories at all of her beginning in South Carolina.

It is amazing that she was unable to glean from her mother's account of their exodus from South Carolina that interaction with her father was a dangerous proposition for her mother; still, she did not. She was simply a starry-eyed little girl who wanted her Daddy.

Life Mark: Heritage

Isaiah Jr.

Mary's interactions with her father were more desired than realized.

Isaiah Jr., nicknamed BayBee, was the youngest of seven children and the only male child. Even his twin sister was older than he. His father, was a full-blooded Native American whose tribal home is somewhere in the region of Akron, Georgia. BayBee's family so "spoiled" the only male child that he never learned to respect anyone, not even himself. Etta later adopted this philosophy of special treatment for the only male child and so inadvertently "hindered" her only son.

In an attempt to halt this gender madness, Mary brought her sons up to be responsible, free-thinking adults. She taught them to cook, clean, wash, iron, and though neither is any good at sewing, they both tried. She did not want them to marry as a remedy to their daily care. She taught them about who they are and helped them to recognize their strengths. These are parenting skills that she gained by learning about her father. She has been known to say, "A bad example is better than no example."

At her father's going home service in early 2007, Mary was amazed at how healthy he looked, considering he had spent his entire adult life as an alcoholic.

He earned a living by driving eighteen-wheelers. As his family tells it, he could be as "drunk as a skunk" and still operate those trucks with precision. Mary never took pride in such bragging. She knew his actions to be irresponsible. From the age of twelve she worried that he might be involved in a serious accident behind the wheel which might take his life and/or the life of an innocent.

One particular story told by Etta relates the sentiment of this chapter. The story told of a time when she had decided to leave her husband. Mary was a toddler and her brother was an infant at the time. Apparently, Etta planned to leave in the middle of the night, while he was asleep. During the day, while he was away from the house (probably at work) Etta packed up some of her and the children's clothing and hid them in the woods close to their home.

Unfortunately for Etta, BayBee realized the clothes were missing and insisted on knowing where they were. While Etta refused to provide the information, Mary kept pointing at a location through the window and announcing, "They're in the woods, Daddy." Her father did not acknowledge her response, but after wearing down his wife to reveal the location of the clothes, he turned to look at Mary and said, "That baby kept saying they were in the woods."

Considering how little contact she had with her father, it could hardly be said that Mary was a daddy's girl; only that she wanted to be.

Mary first remembers seeing her father when she was twelve years old. She had finagled her way into spending the summer in her birthplace, with a relative. Having questioned the relative regarding the whereabouts of her father and expressing the desire to know him, the relative had located and arranged a meeting with her father.

She was so happy, yet so disappointed. You see, no one had ever told her that her father had a problem. She was shocked to learn her father was susceptible to alcohol. He had the bad gene and she worried for him, as well as herself. Had she inherited that gene? She also wondered whether the alcohol gene is the same gene that leads to drug abuse.

Meeting her father at the age of twelve was both a positive and negative *Life Mark* for Mary. She developed an aversion to alcohol that summer. Later, she would happily discover that aside from having a low tolerance, she found the taste of alcohol to be deplorable. During the early 70s she discovered that she has an aversion to marijuana as well. Thank God!

Mary's aversion to alcohol and drugs is probably more mental than physical and it is clearly due to the effects the stuff had on her father. As a commercial driver of big rigs he should have lived a better life.

His use of alcohol was all encompassing and controlling. When he was inebriated he was a loud, insufferable and intolerable drunk. Mary saw this on a couple of occasions when she arrived in South Carolina unannounced. She would just show up at the home of one of her father's sisters.

If he were not in the aunt's home the aunt would ensure that the family located BayBee to inform him of her arrival. Mary suspected that her aunts threatened him; telling him that he had better sober up while she was there, or else.

Once sober, he would locate and sit with his daughter, but he was actually shy around her. He would hold conversations with other family members who were present, but barely venture to ask her a question or two about what was happening in her life. He seemed to be pleased when she would volunteer information and she captured a sense of pride in his demeanor when she would regale him with her most recent accomplishments.

Still, it would have done her heart good to have heard him verbally express his sentiments.

❧ · | · ❧

Peppered with unfulfilled relationships and desires, Mary was not content with her life. Often she pondered the age-old question of heredity versus environment. She felt that her personal experience leaned toward the environment. Even though an individual possesses the genes of the family to which he or she is born, the interaction or lack thereof with those very people is extremely important. Having felt disconnected from both her parents was a very prevalent factor in the development of the person she became.

A homebody at heart, Mary did not interact well with others on a personal level; although her communication skills were more than adequate on a business level. Consequently, she would rather be alone whenever possible. She actually felt disconnected from the rest of the world. Thus, many people have been quick to point out the fact that she is different.

There were plenty of opportunities for Mary to develop a loving relationship with a man, but she usually sabotaged those opportunities without understanding why she had done so. For many years she found it impossible to verbalize her feelings or desires. Consequently, she would allow her partner to guide the relationship. She would listen to his plans for their future then convince herself that what he wanted was not what she wanted and break off the relationship.

Sabotaging her relationships was a subconscious event. It took her a couple of decades to realize what she was doing as she began asking herself why she did not develop a strong relationship with any of the men she met during her twenties. Many of them were good men, though not all.

The lack of a relationship with her father weighed heavily on her heart but more than that, it left her devoid of the knowledge to build a personal relationship with a man.

Etta

Floating throughout the maternal side of Mary's family is a photograph of her grandmother. Were it not for the clothing of the era, one would be hard-pressed to determine whether it was a photograph of her grandmother (Coral), mother (Etta), or of Mary herself.

She will never know whether her mother had regrets over the cards she was dealt in life, but Mary surely regretted those cards on her mother's behalf. To begin with, Etta's mother, Coral, was lost to her children while Etta was still an infant.

Etta's father, Paul, whose nickname was Duck, worked with the railroads. Coral repeatedly established home base in several East Coast cities during the first years of their marriage in order to accommodate her husband's work, but with each addition to the family it became less and less feasible. Since Duck's job kept him on the road, Coral was effectively a single parent.

Additionally, it has been said that Duck was quite a ladies' man, too much so. Eventually, Coral made the decision to return home to South Carolina to rear the children in a stable home and await her husband's visits, when he was able.

Even though Coral had eight children, she was still sought after. To relate a story told by one of Mary's uncles, he remembers (even though he was no more than five years old) being on the front porch of their home in South Carolina. There were two men present. As a car was spotted coming up the road, one man said to the other, "Who is that?" Both men craned their necks to see who was behind the wheel of the vehicle, then one announced rather loudly, "That's Duck!," after which both men ran off into the woods.

Coral's popularity was a source of female envy. On one particular occasion, shortly after giving birth to Etta, two women, known to the family, fought with Coral. One of them held her while the other stabbed her with a knife. It is said that the woman with the knife was interested in a man who had turned his attention to Coral.

According to Coral's eldest daughter who, at the tender age of fifteen, tended to her mother's knife wound, the wound was not serious, but the infection was deadly.

Coral lost her life to jealousy.

❧ · | · ❧

Etta and four of her seven siblings were divided amongst Coral's sisters and brothers. It is perplexing that Duck did not come to get his children, for he was still alive and actively employed with the railroads. The three oldest boys were close enough to adult age that they assumed responsibility for themselves. It is believed that the choice was that of the older boys, but no one is certain because they never spoke of it.

Etta and the eldest girl were placed with one of Coral's brothers and his wife.

Etta revealed but a little of her young life to her children. She told of being approximately six years old when she began walking around her uncle's property in search of cigarette butts on the ground, which she would then pick up and smoke. She did not tell of filching cigarettes, but certainly that is a part of the untold story.

Etta smoked all her life. Consequently, her children breathed tobacco filled air all their lives and Mary began applying it directly to her lungs when she was seventeen years old. Yes, she is currently a smoker, and so are her siblings.

Another important story of Etta's childhood deals with a pet. Her age at the time is unknown but she was still an adolescent when on one occasion Etta was unable to locate her pet chicken. Worried that her pet may have "gotten away," she spent quite some time looking for it and calling out to it before she heard her aunt, whom she called "Mama," call her in to dinner. To her great dismay, she discovered that her pet was displayed on the table as dinner. Etta did not eat chicken that night or since. She would later prepare meals of chicken for her children, but would not partake.

On an occasion during Etta's teenage years, she was seated in the back of the congregation on one Sunday morning, talking and laughing with her boyfriend. Etta's uncle (the uncle who raised her) was in the pulpit and, annoyed by the disturbance she was making, said to her, "Etta, why don't you stand up and tell me and the congregation what is so funny?"

Etta told her children that she gathered her courage, stood up and spoke, "I don't think it's any of your and the congregation's business."

She told of receiving a right good beating that night.

❧ · | · ❧

Before the infamous redevelopment of the southwest area of Washington, DC, which was quite a shake-up for those who were relocated, Etta and her children resided in the home of one of Etta's brothers, on Union Street in the southwest section of the city.

Southwest is the smallest section of Washington, DC. It is located in the half of the city which was donated by the state of Virginia in order to create the nation's Capitol. The other half was, of course, donated by the state of Maryland. The

Potomac River originally flowed through the Southwest section but, when the governmental leadership did not want to spend further monies to develop the last of the swamp land they returned the land on the opposite side of the Potomac River to the state of Virginia, thereby breaking the diamond shape and decreasing the Southwest section of the city. Since the city of Washington, DC owned but one side of the land banks of the Potomac, that waterfront property was highly valued. Thus, the infamous redevelopment and relocation was undertaken.

Prior to the redevelopment, Mary's uncles occupied two two-story houses that were situated side-by-side on the corner of Union Street. Mary assumed the uncles owned the houses, but in this family children were never apprised of such things; not that they thought to ask.

It was a neat little family unit. Etta, her children, and her man, Jude, resided in the home of Etta's brother, Horace and his family; plus, her brother Timmy and his family lived next door. Except for Mary and her siblings, all of the children who lived at home were teenagers and Mary liked being amongst them. It was comforting and very nurturing.

Life Mark: Devastation

Her name was Bella Annette. Bella was eight months old, Mary was approximately four years old. Mary held her aunt's hand as they walked up the hill toward a tent-like structure. It was the aunt who had tended to the knife wound of the grandmother Mary would never get to know. Mary asked of her aunt, "Why did they put Bella in a shoe box?"

They were attending interment services at Mt. Olivet Cemetery in Washington, DC.

ॐ · | · ॐ

Mary, Isaiah III and Bella were in a home that was unfamiliar. They were in a room in the back of the house. The door to the room was open, revealing a partial view of what Mary assumed to be the living room, or parlor room, as it may have been called.

Etta, not wanting to be a burden upon the then named Welfare system found a job and a babysitter to look after her three children while she went to work. The timelines are not exact but Mary was a preschooler and it is guesstimated that she was approximately four, maybe three years old. Mary's younger brother, Isaiah, is one year and four months younger than she.

She was so very young that her memories are fragmented. In addition to Etta's three children, there were three boys present. Presumably they were also in the care of the babysitter. Two of the boys were older and larger than Mary, but they could not have been more than nine or ten years old. The third boy was closer to her brother's age. The three boys may have been brothers because the two younger boys took orders from the eldest.

Through the open door Mary saw a woman leaving the home. During her sleepless nights she could recall the woman's movement about six feet beyond the open door to the room the children occupied. She saw the woman walk towards the door and reach for the doorknob, open the door and walk through it. She could not, however, recall exactly what the woman looked like. In her mind's eye she saw a tall woman of average build (wearing a dress size 10 or 12) with a short bob haircut. The amount of time that passed between the woman's exit and the initiation of the assault is unknown.

The eldest boy told Mary to lie down in the tent which had been built in the corner of the room from a blanket thrown over some sort of rope. Instinctively, Mary responded, "No."

She was physically forced to her hands and knees and beaten across her buttocks with a belt by the eldest boy. He also ordered his brothers to take turns beating her. At some point during the attack her dress was pulled up and the eldest boy climbed onto her back.

Later, the eldest boy ordered his two brothers to climb up the side of the crib in which the baby lay sleeping and jump on her. It was obviously an attack upon females. Many nightmares would be born of the boy's most arduous order to his younger counterparts, "Jump on her head."

At a later stage in life, sometime in her early 40s, she realized, with great surprise, that she does not trust men. Why was that such a surprise?

ᔑ · | · ᔑ

There exists amongst Mary's memories of that incident, a separate memory of an office, perhaps a medical office or a police station:

A man walked her into a back room, closed the door, then placed his hand under her dress, pulled her panties aside and touched her inappropriately. He then walked her back into the outer room where Etta was waiting and informed her that there had not been penetration during the attack. Which attack?!

ᔑ · | · ᔑ

When Mary attempted to talk with her mother or ask questions about that day she was met with tears and dismissal. Etta had lost her baby. She did not seem to realize that Mary and Isaiah had lost their sister and been attacked, or that they needed help. Mary's inability to communicate with her mother would become permanent. Even as an adult, Mary's attempts to converse seriously with her mother extracted only anger or disregard, regardless of the subject matter.

Mary's ability to survive came shortly following Bella's funeral. Unable to sleep at night because of the painful events replaying in her head and the lack of communication regarding the events surrounding her sister's death, she learned to force the memories from her conscious mind. (Of course, at the time she thought she was throwing them away forever.) She would reuse this "erase it" ability throughout her life. She simply forced her mind to expel anything bad or embarrassing from her consciousness and it would cease to exist. It simply never happened. Specifically, she would concentrate on moving an unwanted memory to a specific blank location in her mind, and soon it would no longer existed.

This was, for a child, an ingenious method of survival – but the memories could return. Sometimes, if a memory was particularly devastating, it would be persistent and she would have to move that memory into oblivion a couple of times before it would stay lost. Later, it seemed to be more a process of deliberately forgetting, but she could still accomplish the loss of an unwanted memory well into maturity.

The returned memories of her sister's death are fragmented, but the fragments are clear. They returned following her mother's death. There are still no answers, but now she can analyze the effects that turn of events had upon her subconscious and how she has been unwittingly guided by those events from her subconscious. Those and other suppressed memories played a great part in shaping the person she became.

People sometimes characterize Mary as strange, to which she responds, "I am who I am."

~ · | · ~

The process of placing memories out-of-mind in order to move forward with one's life was, for Mary, necessary. However, in her latter years she came to recognize some unforeseen consequences.

In general, her memory is defective.

If you get her to promise to keep a secret for you, she will most likely keep that secret for about six months to a year. After that period of time, she has most likely forgotten the promise; but if luck is on your side she has forgotten the secret as well.

If you and she are holding a general conversation, the chances that she will remember the majority of the conversation for greater than four hours is approximately 70%; greater than two weeks, approximately 30%. She has always admired people who can remember a conversation, then years later repeat it verbatim.

Mary has difficulty remembering people's names. She discovered that by creating a nickname she is more likely to remember that person's name. Sometimes she actually calls the person by the nickname she has given them, but most often not. Providing a nickname is her method of remembering that person's name. On many an occasion she has felt embarrassed because she is aware that she should remember someone's name but it just will not come to her. It happens with family members as well as with friends and acquaintances.

Later in life, Mary birthed two sons. She made the mistake (or perhaps it was a good thing) of naming them similarly, their first names rhyme and the spelling alters only the first letter. She called them by the wrong name so often that when they were young children they would sometimes agree to switch names for a day because they assumed she would use the wrong name anyway. Sometimes she got it right – poor kids.

While Mary has the ability to learn quickly, she is just as likely to lose the majority of that information two weeks later to some dark corner of her mind. A meter that measures level of interest would probably determine which information gets retained.

She has created a habit of writing things down or placing them into her computer in an attempt to prevent data loss. It is helpful, though not infallible.

Life Mark: Puppeteers

Mary formed a very clear memory of her first day at school. It was an unwelcome assault upon her little world. Her mother held her by the hand as they left the house and walked up the street toward Greenleaf Elementary School.

If there was any prior discussion of the fact that she would be attending school, her memory did not capture it. She wondered where she was being taken and whether she would ever return. She thought she was being given away.

They arrived at a large building filled with children and were directed to a specific room. As they entered the room together, a woman approached them. The woman introduced herself as the teacher. Mary watched as her mother held a short conversation with the woman, after which her mother took her by the hand to guide her to a desk.

Etta told her that she would be back to pick her up and Mary breathed a sigh of relief. At least she was not going to leave her there forever. Her mother slipped quietly out of the room. She watched her leave, then took a long look around, realized that she did not know anyone there and felt panic.

The teacher directed the children to be quiet as she checked the roll. She called each name on her list, but when she called out the name Mary, no one answered. She called the name several times, with no response. The teacher continued down the list and when she reached the end she asked if there was anyone whose name was not called. Etta's daughter raised her hand.

The teacher said, "Well, you must be Mary."

"No," she said. "My name is Ruth."

"No dear, Ruth is your middle name. It's listed right here. Your first name is Mary." There was laughter from the rest of the class.

"No it's not! My name is Ruth!" As far as she knew her name was Ruth; that is what the entire family called her. Not only did she have to deal with this strange location, strange woman and lots of strange kids, but now she had to deal with this strange name as well. She was not a happy camper.

"Okay," the teacher replied.

The other children launched into animated play amid lots of chatter. She felt out of place. Shortly thereafter, she realized no one was paying any attention to her and that she could probably leave without being noticed; off she went.

When she arrived at home no one answered the door, so she sat down on the step in front of the door and waited for someone to return home and let her in.

She was startled by her mother's voice, "Ruth! What are you doing here?"

She noted the use of what she knew to be the correct name and said, "I left."

Etta smiled and with her arms filled with groceries she unlocked the door and they entered. Together they put away the groceries as Etta explained to her daughter that she would have to return to school.

Etta laughed deeply when her daughter told of the roll call experience.

Through laughter she said, "Your first name is Mary, but we call you by your middle name."

"Don't you think you should have told me what my name is," she asked.

Continuing to laugh, Etta informed her daughter that it had simply never occurred to her that she did not know her full name.

When the task at hand was complete Etta again took her by the hand and they made the dreaded walk for the second time that day.

The teacher expressed relief at having located a lost child and vowed to keep a closer eye on her. Mary knew that any future escape would be far more difficult, though not impossible. However, it would be a futile operation if her mother was simply going to bring her back.

Mary settled down and decided to make the best of the situation. Apparently she learned to love her teacher, for when her mother gave birth to another little girl she insisted that the baby bear her teacher's name. Mary's youngest sister bears the teacher's first name, Sharon, as her middle name.

❧ · | · ❧

Anyone who has spent a significant amount of time in the nation's Capital is only too aware of the fact that the political machine runs on campaign contributions and corresponding promises. Our governmental leadership, federal and municipal, is peppered with incompetent individuals who have in some way or another extracted political power by way of the weaknesses in our political system.

The system allows for the advancement of leadership who are less than competent, as well as for individuals whose morals have been corrupted by the desire for money. Hopefully, the most intelligent government and private leadership will soon institute testing procedures for management levels. Management has certainly created enough testing for lower level workers, yet they have conspicuously ignored the same consideration for themselves and their cronies. They simply do not care, and the public does not call them on it often enough.

Washington DC launched a redevelopment plan. As presented to the residents, the plan was to temporarily relocate the current residents, tear down the existing structures and build a new community; then the relocated citizens would return. Right! In actuality the plan was to create a revenue generating epicenter at the Potomac riverfront property and the only interest in the existing residents was to get them out of the way.

Thus, Mary began second grade in a new school. Both Etta's brothers were offered homes in separate communities while Etta and her children received occupancy in a two-bedroom apartment in the Lincoln Heights government housing project in the northeast section of the city. The family had been separated and spread far apart.

Mary believes many of America's problems stem from its abandonment of the extended family structure.

The end of Etta's relationship with Jude went unnoticed by the children. Mary does not recall ever being in his presence in their new Lincoln Heights home though she definitely remembers the existence of a close bond between her mother and the father of her two sisters while on Union Street. She remembers quiet conversations and lots of giggling between Etta and Jude. She can only speculate that he disappeared from their lives as a result of the welfare department's "no man aboard" policy. He may have been forced to live elsewhere.

Lincoln Heights was a collection of people with low or no income. Very few households contained fathers, though some households contained men (some of them with changing faces).

Etta received public assistance. It was referred to as "Welfare." There were periodic deliveries of food from the government stores. Specifically, there was some sort of canned "mystery" meat which many can yet identify. The meat was minced, packed tight into a can, and then some sort of oil was poured in to fill out the volume of the can and probably to preserve the meat as well. The cans were sized rather large, much more than a family of four could consume in one or two meals and there were often multiple containers of this meat in the freezer section of Etta's refrigerator. Etta's children did not like this meat, and it was always left for those times when the stomach, out of hunger, would accept anything.

The food deliveries also included large cans of peanut butter in which the oil had separated, as well as blocks of unsliced cheese. The can of peanut butter required constant stirring upon opening, to reintegrate approximately 1½ inches of oil that was resting on the top. It often took an hour or so to reintegrate the oil into the peanut butter.

Also during their early years at Lincoln Heights, there were visits from "Welfare" representatives when they would search the home to ensure that no "man" lived with them. (This process is no longer utilized by the current public assistance program.)

Such were the indignities suffered by individuals for having the gall to be poor. Why is it that people are judged not by their character but by their means? Some of the most awful people Mary ever met were people of great means, with minimal character.

So, they were a single-parent household, living in government housing and surviving by use of government assistance in the form of a monthly check and food handouts. It was a very degrading existence because those in charge of providing assistance performed their paid duties with contempt. There was little graciousness or compassion. So much more could have been accomplished with smiles and kind words. Instead, at every turn, the goal was to make people feel as though they were worthless – the system was just plain evil.

⟶ · | · ⟶

After the move to Lincoln Heights Mary was enrolled in second grade at Merritt Elementary School. It was a school long past its prime and Mary will always have a vivid memory of plaster falling from the ceiling, upon her and her fellow students as they were being marched through the hallways.

It was amid this crumbling school that Mary forged friendships with two girls in her class, Alissa and Evette. The duo enveloped Mary into their existing friendship and the three of them became inseparable friends for life.

At the beginning of the following school year Aiton Elementary School opened its doors. The newly formed trio of friends shared classes from third through sixth grades there. It was basically an enjoyable experience and it was at Aiton that Mary discovered an aptitude for academic learning.

The three girls shared a thirst for knowledge and each provided healthy unspoken challenges for the other two. Each was from a single parent home in Lincoln Heights, and the girls' mothers each separately approved of their friendship. The mothers liked that their daughters were associating with intelligent, quiet, "good girls."

The trio often speculated about what their mothers would think if they could listen in on their conversations or somehow view their behavior when they were not in the presence of one of the mothers.

Together, the girls experienced their first drink of alcohol, sitting at the top of the thirty foot hill behind the apartment building where Mary lived with her family. There was a six foot wide dirt path directly in front of them. The hill was regularly used as a short cut path to the junior high school below and was so steep that the end of the downhill climb was always accomplished at a forced run.

Evette had managed to sneak a pint of alcohol from her older brother and the girls decided to learn about the effects of alcohol for themselves.

"What kind is it?" Mary asked.

"It's rum. My brother says rum and cola tastes good, but I had to get out of the house as fast I could so we don't have any cola."

"It doesn't matter, we can just drink it like it is," came Alissa's encouragement. She always provided the bravado.

Within minutes the girls were enjoying a giggle-fest, then the alcohol told them it would be a good idea to roll down the hill. Now positioned at the bottom of the hill, the giggles grew louder as the girls recognized the ridiculousness of the adventure while they brushed the dirt from their hair and clothing. As they sat at the bottom of the hill, waiting for the effects of the alcohol to wear off, they knew without saying that they would never repeat the adventure.

The girls determined that alcohol produces stupid ideas. The ascertained information would be filed away under "now we know," and new adventures would be sought.

Life Mark: Vulnerability

An examination of Etta's life during the Lincoln Heights phase would reveal that she was a woman desperate to locate her soul mate. Her initial selection, Mary and Isaiah's father, was obviously a great disappointment because she put greater than 400 miles between them. Curiously, she never formally divorced her husband, nor did she revert to the use of her maiden name.

Jude, her second choice and the father of her third and fourth children, had disappeared from her life by the time Etta reached Lincoln Heights.

As you might well imagine, a woman alone with children is vulnerable and often preyed upon. Amongst her boyfriends Cory and Felix stand out most, for the wrong reasons.

Cory was his first name, his last name is lost in the dark areas of Mary's memory, if she ever knew it. He was a construction worker, but, most importantly, he owned a car. The children liked Cory to visit because he would pack the entire family into the car and take them for a ride. They were easy to please.

It was not very long, maybe three or four months, before Cory moved into their home. Mary was very pleased to have the appearance of a complete family. Shortly thereafter, she learned from first-hand experience to *be careful of what you wish for.*

She was ten years old. Etta had found a job as a dishwasher at a hotel in downtown D.C. It was an evening position and Cory would pick up Etta from work at night. One evening Cory asked Mary to ride with him to pick up her mother from work. Her sister and brother wanted to go as well, but Cory said they should get ready for bed and they would be back soon.

It was the first time Mary had been allowed to ride in the front seat of the car. Cory was silent and she was pleased, it allowed her to soak up the beauty of downtown Washington, D.C., with so many beautiful lights against the night sky. They were stopped at a traffic light. Cory reached over and placed his hand under her skirt. She jumped in fear. What was he doing? She closed her legs tight together, but did not say anything. She was afraid.

He said, "Open you legs, baby."

She held her legs tight together, but still said nothing. She was frozen in place. The traffic light changed, he removed his hand and the car moved on toward her mother. Oh God, how she wanted to see her mother.

They arrived at the hotel and Etta approached the car.

She said, "Ruth, what are you doing here? Get in the back."

With a chilling command Cory emphatically stated, "No, don't you move!" With animosity in his voice he then said to Etta, "*You* get in the back!"

Mary thought, "*What's happening?*" Again, her mother directed her to get into the back of the car and again Cory dared her to do so.

She was so scared. She had thought that her mother's presence would cause Cory to return to his normal behavior, but instead he had become vicious with her mother. Now she was afraid for both herself and her mother.

Mary tucked her head down, balled up into a knot and did not move. Her mother got into the back and there was no conversation in the car on the way home. When the car arrived at home Mary could not get out of it fast enough. She vowed never to get back into that car!

Somehow or another Etta and Cory's relationship survived that evening. Mary lived in fear. There would be another, more traumatic experience for Mary before Etta and Cory's relationship would come to an abrupt end.

Even though Mary preferred being indoors she began spending more time outside of the apartment when Cory was there. She was disgusted by him and could not even stand to smell him. She learned to duck and dodge around him to insure they were never alone.

Cory became desperate and bold enough to attempt to rape her in the presence of the other two children while their mother was at work. Even though he was unsuccessful Mary felt the sting of fear and vulnerability and, still timid about talking to her mother, she was thankful that her brother had the courage she searched for and told their mother of the attempt.

Etta and Cory had a big fight that night. While Etta yelled for her children to stay in their bedroom, they fought physically and Cory got the best of the fight, but Etta rebuked his attempts to sweet-talk her afterward and demanded that he move out of her home immediately. Later, the three children did all they could to doctor Etta's black eye and assure her that they could survive without Cory's car and the extra income he brought into the home.

Amazingly, Etta never talked with Mary about the fight or the preceding event. Mary needed to hear that she was not to blame. She needed some understanding of why her mother's boyfriend tried to take advantage of her. She needed to know how to tell which men were worth a woman's time and effort and which were not. She wanted to hear from her mother that it was not her fault that her mother's relationship had failed. She just needed to hear something from her mother. Nothing said. The divide between mother and daughter was deepened.

Later that night, amid a darkened bedroom, Mary was unable to sleep. While her brother and sister slept with audible breaths, she set about moving her mother's ex-boyfriend into the dark recesses of her mind. As she finally closed her eyes and fell into restful rejuvenation, he no longer existed.

Cory was blamed, though never charged, for a later break-in; the only thing taken was the color television which he had bought for the family about a month before his precipitous departure. There was no proof, but it was in keeping with his character.

Etta had other boyfriends after Cory, but thankfully there were no more baby predators. There was only one other physical fight. By that time Mary was twelve years old and she was sick of her family being seen as victims and treated as less than others.

Remembering the beating her mother endured at Cory's hands, she refused to stay in the room as her mother directed. Instead, she went in search of a weapon and found a small ball peen hammer. As she entered the living room, she saw her mother lying on the floor being straddled by her current boyfriend, Felix, as he was punching downward toward her face. Bang! The sound of the hammer striking his back was startling. To Mary's surprise her mother yelled at her, "Ruth, don't kill him!"

Her brother asked, "Why did you do that, Ruth?"

She looked upon her younger sister's face to see fear in her wide eyes.

The only emotion Mary felt was relief; relief that this man was no longer beating on her mother. The surprised reaction of her mother and siblings made her question whether she was any longer capable of empathy.

She had simply done what she had to do.

Life Mark: Reverence

Etta was reared in church every Sunday and, therefore, particularly because South Carolina is a part of the Bible Belt, it is assumed that she was in church throughout the week as well. For reasons that Mary is unaware, Etta did not bring up her children in the church.

Unknowingly, Mary faced life unprepared. She lacked preparation for the life ahead of her. She knew only that she wanted to be independent; she stepped into her independence with confidence but with no sense of direction.

She was approximately eight years old when she first remembers attending church for the first time. She was in the company of a female cousin who is two years older. It was a true store-front church on "H" Street in the northeast section of Washington, DC.

The girls were seated amongst the congregation. Even though there was minimal seating, they had a choice of seats. The cousin informed Mary that the preacher was a friend to her family. The preacher made an indelible impression upon Mary. He was a nice man; tall and slender with dark skin and a nice smile. He spoke to Mary, a child, in a way that both conveyed and commanded respect – definitely a desirable skill.

Mary was, however, far less impressed with his sermon that day. He preached of hellfire and brimstone, of a God that demanded obedience or else. It was her introduction to church but the kind-hearted man was trying to teach her to fear God.

As meek as she was, she could not accept that point of view. Instinctively she knew that if there was a God, He was not mean. Considering that He is addressed as the Father, the Son and the Holy Spirit, how can He be poised with a hand in the air, waiting to slap down anyone who steps out of line? What is benevolent about that? How could God guide us away from Hell, yet rule His children with meanness? No, the preacher had it wrong and she instinctively knew it. Also, if He were such a punishing God, He would already have removed multitudes for having performed evil deeds. If God were truly a punishing God, how many people would remain on earth; Mary doubted there would be any concerns over the population growth.

Needless to say, she did not return to that church.

Her attempts at reading the Bible on her own were thwarted by her own mind and lack of knowledge. She was unable to read the King James Version of the Bible with fluidity and, therefore, she did not receive a strong enough level of comprehension. In short, she was surviving in this world merely by the way she knew God within her heart, which is far better than He is known by many, yet it was painfully incomplete.

∽ · | · ∼

Mary was standing at the window of the Lincoln Heights bedroom she shared with her sister and brother. The windows of their apartment were positioned high off the ground and their residence was on the ground floor of the three-level apartment building. She was approximately thirteen years old and was not feeling particularly loved at the time. She was in a state of despair.

She had just received another terrible beating at the hands of her mother, this time because her mother mistakenly believed she had ventured into the world of sex. During the beating, Etta had provided a directive, "If you come home pregnant you and that child are going to be living in the streets." Perhaps it was the thought of trying to take care of yet another human being that upset Etta so. Whatever had triggered Etta's disdain, it had also triggered Mary's despair. Standing there at the window with her arms lying on the window ceil and her chin resting on the back of her hands, she wanted to die.

With great concentration she blanked her mind and had every intention of dying right then and there. Unexpectedly, she found herself positioned above the room, looking down upon herself. Then she realized she was not alone.

Jesus was there. He was dressed in a flowing white robe which was embellished with gold, and although His physical features could be described, there would be no purpose for He could well choose different appearances for others. He communicated with Mary directly. Try as she might, she could not remember the conversation, even immediately thereafter. However, she distinctly remembers the feeling of love and hope that He instilled in her. She had a newfound self-confidence.

She returned to her body and no conscious decision was required to abandon all thoughts of dying; the thoughts no longer existed. She has called upon that experience several times over the years; it is a constant and immutable source of hope. She has even tried, unsuccessfully, to recreate the experience. She wants to stand in His presence every day. That desire is selfish and yet, it is also true.

She never shared her experience with anyone. It was much later in life before she heard the phrase "out-of-body experience." Out-of-body experiences were being attributed only to people who survived near death experiences in the operating room, but she knew better.

Life Mark: Independence

Mary often fantasized about having been reared in her birth place in South Carolina, instead of Washington, DC. Whether reared by one parent or two, she thought her life would have been richer.

As a resident of the Lincoln Heights housing project, Mary came to realize that large numbers of peopled gathered together in one place is detrimental to human development. Consider the adage "one bad apple spoils the whole barrel." That adage applies whether the barrel contains 5 or 5,000.

Apartment living is particularly undesirable. A cursory examination reveals people stacked atop people. How could that ever be good?

Mary dreamed of the opportunity to build her perfect dream home. It's most prominent feature would be it's solitude, in a location where she could stand on the roof, make a 360° turn and not be able to see her next door neighbor.

She has always been quick to admit that she is not a people person. Earlier in life she tried to be a people pleaser. It was not a conscious decision, but was probably born of the desire to be liked. At any rate, she quickly discovered that the more she did to make people like her, the more they asked of her and, in some cases, the more they despised her.

In short order she learned to just be herself and to allow people their opinions, whatever they may be.

At Kelly Miller Junior High School the trio was separated. The DC school system used a track system at the time. All the sixth graders of the area elementary schools sat for a placement exam. The first thirty students with the highest scores were placed in class 7-1, and the consecutive classes were filled until the last class had been designated. Evette tested into 7-2, while Mary and Alissa were placed into 7-3. Initially, Evette complained about her teachers and classmates; but when Alissa and Mary teased her that she was too smart for them she buckled down to perform well in class and take solace in the fact that she could spend her after school hours with her friends.

The school was situated at the bottom of the hill behind the apartment building in which Mary lived. It was an easy walk to school. Living furthest away, Evette would collect Alissa, then the two would head off to collect Mary and rush her to get ready so they would not be late.

While in the eighth grade, Mary's brother was in seventh grade and their mother attended adult progressive training classes to become a secretary. The three of them attended Kelly Miller at the same time. It was a difficult time for the two preteens, Isaiah in particular. The slightest infraction caused the teachers to deliver Isaiah to his mother for instant behavioral correction.

Still, the two teenagers were proud of their mother's efforts and her determination to become completely independent. Etta's quest for independence was absorbed by all three of her children.

Etta did well in her classes, received a certificate of completion and began completing applications for employment with the U.S. government. Mary was honored to assist in the process of typing applications and, of course, she was quite pleased that her education would continue unhindered by her mother's on-site presence.

Soon thereafter Etta was hired as a secretary at the Department of State. Her elation infected the entire household.

Life Mark: Chaos

Life felt better in Etta's household after she became a federal government employee. Financially, the family did not take very many steps forward because an entry level secretarial salary was barely enough to replace the lost welfare assistance. However, there was a better sense of self throughout the household and, luckily, Etta continued to qualify for public housing, though she was required to begin paying a small amount of rent. There was also an expectation of future monetary increases, something which did not exist in the assistance program.

Etta impressed upon her children the importance of their assistance by way of self-sufficiency and staying out of trouble. She had not entrusted her children to babysitters following the loss of Bella Annette. She chose instead to charge the children with their own care, while having neighbors look out for them.

The neighboring women were only too happy to help out one of their own who was about to climb out of the system. The only babysitting options Etta considered were family members, which she utilized when she went out for a night of entertainment.

The two younger children were directed to follow the instructions of their older sister. Mary was charged with keeping the other two in line; it was a job which she did not embrace. While she was quiet and reserved, both her siblings were outgoing and rambunctious. She found it nearly impossible to control them.

When Etta was upset with Mary she addressed her daughter by her full name: first, middle and last; but when she was truly angry Etta would call Mary by her father's name, usually just before she hit her.

There were many occasions when Mary took a physical beating for something one or both her younger siblings had done; even when it was obvious that the younger children had performed the infraction, Mary was told that she was responsible because she was the oldest. While beating children is now widely considered child abuse, in the fifties and sixties it was considered parental prerogative; nothing was said about it; the consequences were either unknown or undocumented.

While Etta was establishing her place within the governmental workforce Mary and Alissa graduated Junior High School, into Spingarn Senior High School. Evette had been accepted into McKinley Technical High School. All three girls were forced to utilize public bus transportation back and forth to school. Because Evette had a further distance to travel, she was required to leave home much earlier. Mary and Alissa saw less and less of her, but managed to keep in touch by way of telephone and weekend adventures.

Catching the bus was quite an adjustment for Mary, since time management had never been her strong suit. It became a problem for Mary because missing a bus could mean she would be twenty minutes late for school; whereas, if behind schedule when she was walking to school she could run and either get there on time or just a couple of minutes late.

Believe it or not, the offending infraction often occurred because she was reading late into the night. Mary had always been a night child. Being sent to bed early more often meant extra time for her to read or to allow her mind to wander, rather than obtaining extra sleep. Several times Etta had busted Mary with a book and flashlight as she was reading under the covers, well beyond her bedtime.

All three girls had developed a love for the Nancy Drew series while they were still in elementary school. If they were lucky enough to come across a Nancy Drew book at the public library on Central Avenue that they had not read, they would pass the book amongst themselves before returning it to the library. Adventure novels were the personal choice of all three.

Even considering the challenges of time management Mary managed to do well in high school. As a senior in junior high school she had pre-selected her classes for the first semester of high school. Not being fond of history classes (she loved the story telling portion of class, but often had difficultly matching names, dates and events), she had elected to take a mechanical drawing class instead. She thought it would be a lot more fun than history class.

On her first day as a high school student she was introduced to the slow, deep, smooth voice of the school's Principal as he addressed the new students in the school's auditorium. He addressed them as tenth graders. They were each assigned a homeroom class where they would spend the first forty-five minutes of each day. Homeroom classes were gender specific, either male or female. It was not a credited class, but Mary was quite pleased to have a forty-five minute allotment in which to complete the prior days' homework assignments.

From then on the daily routine began with the Principal's voice breezing through the classroom speakers as he made the morning announcements over the intercom system. He always began, "Good morning seniors, juniors and tenth graders . . ." She felt an immediate assault at being addressed as a tenth grader, as did the majority of the tenth grade class. Immediately, the greeting conveyed the fact that they were nothing until they became juniors. Each and every day the announcements began this way and for Mary it was an added incentive to succeed.

She and Alissa had been assigned different homeroom classes. Mary could not wait to meet her teachers and report back to Alissa at the end of the day as they would make comparisons in each other's experience. Each student had been provided with a computer printout of their class schedule and as Mary progressed through the day she was quite pleased. Her teachers were all very pleasant and she became assured that she could accomplish the work.

The expectations were, of course, greater than what she had become accustomed to at Kelly Miller, but she was certain she could keep up. As the school day neared its end, she located her final class, mechanical drawing, and stopped short at the door. A look through the door's inset glass window revealed an entire class of boys. *"What have I done,"* she asked herself. History class was looking a lot better; maybe it was not too late to change.

The male teacher opened the door and said to her, "You must be Mary, come on in."

"Nope." Her cursory look through the glass had revealed a classroom of tall drafting tables and the only vacant table was smack dab in the center of the classroom. There were far too many boys for Mary, who was still very shy. She had no desire to be in that classroom.

Recognizing her trepidation, the teacher directed the boy seated nearest the door to move to the empty drafting table in the center of the classroom. Mary acquiesced and placed her books on the large drafting table nearest the door; she could escape if need be.

As he described the course work and his expectations of his students, Mary was glad she had entered the class. It would be a fun class and, best of all, there would be no homework assignments.

As she caught up with Alissa after the last bell, she could not wait to tell her of the mistake she had made in her schedule.

"Alissa, when I elected mechanical drawing I didn't realize it was a class normally taken by boys. I may have to switch to history class."

"It doesn't sound like it would be a boys only class, Mary. It sounds like a prerequisite for becoming an architect and there are plenty of female architects."

Mary stretched her body length upward and emphatically stated, "Yeah, there's nothing about it that seems like it can't be performed by girls and the class work seems easy enough. I think I can do the work just as well as any of the boys in the class."

Alissa laughed and asked, "So, you're not going to change to a history class?"

"No, I think I'm going to prove that girls can do well in this class."

"Good for you," Alissa became her cheerleader.

Mary worked hard in all her classes and took much pride in homeroom class when, after the first quarter grades were posted, her homeroom teacher listed the top grades on the board. Mary watched her homeroom teacher write her name at the top of the board as the teacher posted that she had received four A's and two B's. She was so proud. The rest of the girls in the class were pretty and/or popular and Mary had felt that she did not fit in, but now she had a platform to stand on and was grateful for the girls who bothered to congratulate her.

After the first grading period, Mary was the only member of the mechanical drawing class who had earned an "A." From that point on an intense competition erupted between Mary and the rest of the class, particularly after the teacher pointed out the fact that the only girl in the class received the only "A."

Mary was pleased that the class placed a practical use of geometry into play. Geometry, or rather math, had always been her best subject and she was happy to have a practical application.

Her jubilation over her accomplishment at school was shattered when she proudly presented her report card to her mother and was asked, "Where did these "Bs" come from?"

She thought, "Why should I even try?" Except for her mechanical drawing class, where she was determined to win the competition, her efforts slacked even though she managed to stay on the honor roll and remain a member of the Honor Society during her entire stay at Spingarn.

Etta did not realize the effect her disapproval had upon her daughter and may even have thought she was providing an extra incentive. It is doubtful that a mother would deliberately destroy her child's attempts at success.

Mary wondered whether her mother was punishing her for the loss of her daughter, but was hard pressed to actually ask. She knew the question would not go well for her, regardless of the answer.

Sometime during the first semester of school the Principal's announcement included a call for girls who wanted to join the newly formed Girls Drill Team. Mary thought nothing of the announcement, but Alissa was excited about attending the tryouts and Mary did not hesitate to accompany her girlfriend to the tryouts, though she did not think she would make the team.

Mary and Alissa became members of Spingarn's first Girls Drill Team. The team was actually organized by another student, Jeremy, who was a member of the school's Army R.O.T.C. program and leader of the Boys Drill Team. Jeremy held tryouts for the girls team and hand-selected each member of the team. Initially, he recruited members of the boys drill team to work with the girls as they learned to march and drill. It was a painstaking process but, luckily, Jeremy had the necessary patience. Inside of two months, the girls had become a cohesive unit, working as one.

They were a fourteen-woman team; a three by four woman formation, plus a guide arm bearer who was always positioned to the front and right of the formation, and a leader who called commands. They wore tap shoes and it was very impressive to watch them drill as a unit, yet hear only one sound as fourteen feet hit the wood flooring of the school's armory at once. Had anyone been out of step, it would have been obvious, but they were well-practiced and took great pride in their routines. They were the school "stars."

On Armed Forces Day during Mary's junior year, there was a morning assembly, attended by all students. The Principal introduced the various representatives of the armed services who were there for the purpose of providing the students with information about each branch of the nation's military. Later, the guests would gather in the school's armory to make themselves available for questions.

In the armory, Jeremy had arranged for the Girls Drill Team to perform for the representatives.

The armory shook with great applause from the military representatives and the students. Naturally, the team had access to all of the representatives and Mary made certain to talk to the female representatives from each branch.

She was seriously considering a military career because even though she was an accomplished academic student with partial National Merit and Wellesley College scholarships, her family and she had no money for college. She knew she would feel out of place with people who had money to burn, while she would be scraping together pennies just to cover the cost of her books, not to mention how out of place she felt when interviewed by Wellesley students who were wearing expensive designer clothing that she could never imagine being able to afford. So for her, the military was a very viable solution.

Mary was most impressed by the female representative from the United States Marine Corps, Gunnery Sergeant Jansen. She was a "put together" woman of great confidence. She expressed the Marine Corps' desire to attract people of pride and excellence. Also, since it was the time of the Vietnam war, Mary was happy to hear that Marine Corps women were not sent into combat and, in point of fact, could not be sent anywhere outside of the United States without their very own permission. (Of course, it was the late 1960s/early 1970s; times and rules have changed.)

Mary talked to Gunnery Sergeant Jansen for approximately twenty minutes, after which she knew which branch she would select if, indeed, she decided to travel the military route.

✍ · | · ✌

Toward the end of her junior year at Spingarn, Mary was startled to learn that the family was moving to an apartment complex in southeast Washington, DC. She knew nothing of the area. Apparently, the new location was a three bedroom unit, allowing the girls a separate bedroom from their brother. Mary had just turned sixteen years old and upon reflection realized the inappropriateness of sharing a room with her fourteen year old brother, even though they got along well enough for siblings.

The problem for Mary was that she learned of the move when she arrived at home from school on a Friday afternoon to find her mother home from work and the family already packing. She joined in to help with the task. There was magically a moving truck in front of the apartment building the next morning. Mary did not even have time to call Alissa and Evette to give them a heads up. The family all worked to load up the truck and off they went. As the truck was just beginning to pull away with Mary and Isaiah standing in the back with the door to the truck open, one of her brother's "associates" approached the back of the truck.

The associate shouted, "Good-bye, Mary!"

Perplexed that he would speak to her instead of her brother she responded, "Bye."

"Don't talk to him Ruth," her brother said, loud enough for the "associate" to overhear. Mary never knew why they left their home so abruptly, but she thought it had something do with her brother and his "associates."

The new community, Barnaby Terrace in southeast, was like a different world. They had moved to a private apartment complex which consisted of hard working though low income families. There was a greater number of two-parent households on Barnaby Terrace than in Lincoln Heights but there were still some single parent households.

Barnaby Terrace was configured in a horseshoe shape. Entering the street from Wheeler Road it continued in a U-shape, past two dozen or so apartment buildings until it once again dumped its traffic back onto Wheeler Road. It was a mini-community.

Barnaby Terrace was, however, surrounded by several government housing projects and Mary felt hostility when venturing off the street where they lived. She felt an air of contempt emanating from the project housing; something she had not experienced or recognized in or around the Lincoln Heights project housing where she had grown up. There were some very rough people about and she was afraid, though she had long since learned not to display fear.

For the first few months Mary spent most of her free time talking on the phone with Alissa or Evette, usually Alissa because they shared a common high school experience.

In order to get to school she had to take three different buses and considering that she was time management challenged, she was sent to her counselor's office several times for tardiness.

During one of the times she was sent to her counselor there was a surprise waiting for her. She thought she would be counseled again regarding her tardiness, but she was actually offered a position in the Upward Bound Program.

It was a summer program for high school students who were considered upwardly mobile. It was a unique opportunity to prepare for college while living on the Trinity College campus. Students would live on campus Monday through Friday, and could, if they so chose, return home on the weekends.

Also, each student would receive a weekly stipend of ten dollars, and there was a planned trip to Savannah State University, a four-year university in Savannah, Georgia. Mary happily completed the application form and was accepted.

It was a wonderful opportunity which she enjoyed immensely. It was only spoiled by her mother's announcement that Mary would have to use her ten dollar stipend to purchase her clothing for the coming school year. Independence and responsibility were not fun.

At the start of her senior year, Mary was quite happy to begin her final year of high school, even though her wardrobe was smaller than usual. True to her word, her mother provided no assistance with the purchase of school clothes.

Mary had gathered that money was tighter following the move to Southeast but had no idea just how bad things were. Even though she was disappointed over the situation, she would never question her mother.

After the first week of school Mary was called into her counselor's office. She had thought it to be a preemptive strike against tardiness; she had been very careful to leave home early enough to arrive on time, scheduling a timely arrival even if she managed to miss one of the three buses along the route.

Surprisingly, the counselor informed her that she had learned of Mary's change of address outside of the school's district. The woman further explained to Mary that she would have to transfer to Ballou High School, near her home.

Mary was devastated. How did she find out? "Who told you that?," she asked. The counselor refused to answer. Later that evening, it seemed to Mary as though her own mother took the blame for the betrayal when Etta yelled at her, "Stop complaining, one school is the same as another." She was wrong.

Ballou High School had been in the newspapers for gang fighting and rioting. During the previous school year, more than one student had lost his or her life while on the school grounds. Mary had no desire to attend school there.

To make matters worse, when she arrived there she was assigned classes in typing, shorthand and remedial level English. She protested, informing the registrar that she was an honor roll student in possession of two academic scholarships and needed college bound classes. She was brushed aside and told that they were the only classes available; she could either attend them or not.

Mary was reassured that her opinion of the school was right on point.

Additionally, her challenges with time management were no longer met by meetings with a counselor, but by chain-locked doors. Entry was not allowed to students who arrived late.

The final straw came when she was walking to school with a group of friends from her apartment complex. They were caught in the middle of gunfire as police chased a suspect through a small wooded area which the students used as a shortcut to school. They all dropped to the ground and by the grace of God no one was shot, not even the suspect. When the police saw them on the ground they said nothing.

Mary became a high school dropout in the twelfth grade. Her mother told her she was stupid.

One of Mary's Barnaby Terrace friends had joined the Job Corps as an alternative to living at home. Mary investigated the possibility and learned that Job Corps had a program to ready students for the G.E.D. exam. She was certain she could pass it immediately but she would not be allowed to sit for the exam in Washington, DC until her nineteenth birthday. Job Corps offered to send her to a site in Texas where she could study for the exam and sit for it as soon as she felt she was ready.

Mary's first flight aboard an airplane was provided by the Job Corps to the Dallas/Ft. Worth airport. Her final destination was McKinney, Texas. Three months later she returned to Washington, DC with her G.E.D. and joined the government workforce as a file clerk. She was physically positioned in a Department of Housing and Urban Development warehouse where she would pull requested files to be sent to the main building at

7th and D Streets in southwest. Inside of three months she had been promoted to a typist in one of the many typing pools at the main building. Her eagerness to perform produced two additional promotions within a few short months.

Mary recognized the apathy of her fellow employees in their willingness to put the majority of the work on her desk. Her commitment was so noted that the typing pool's clients would bypass the unit's in-box to bring their work directly to her. She did not mind performing the work, but was disgusted by the behavior of her coworkers, particularly when they would place their work on her desk then flitter off down the hall to flirt with married men.

In March of 1971, Mary walked into her place of work and presented her supervisor with a typed two-week notice of resignation. When the supervisor read the notice, she yelled aloud, "the Marines!"

"That's right," Mary replied.

The shock traveled around the room; it was not so much because she had joined the military, but because she had chosen the Marines. Mary thought it was an odd reaction, but she realized that her coworkers had not researched the military as she had. In Mary's opinion, the Marine Corps' "Do it right or don't do it all" attitude was exactly suited to her personality.

Life Mark: USMC, Parris Island, SC

The recruitment building was on the corner of 11th Street and Pennsylvania Avenue in northwest; five blocks from The White House. The regal presence of the Capitol building was visible just eleven blocks down Pennsylvania Avenue in the opposite direction.

The Marine Corps, Navy, Army and Air Force recruiters were all located in the same building with street level entrance – sectioned off, but not partitioned. It was possible to walk from one recruiter to the next.

As Mary talked to the female Marine Corps recruiter, she was impressed with the recruiter's self-confidence and how neat she looked in her uniform. Her heart dropped as she was informed she would need the signature of a parent because she was only eighteen years old. With dejection in her voice she told the recruiter of her mother's opinion that women in the military were all "dikes" and she did not think her mother would ever agree to sign the papers. Her mother was very possessive and over-protective. Although it was borne of love, Mary thought her mother was stifling her creative abilities.

The recruiter arranged to go to her home to talk with her mother personally. Meanwhile, Mary took a few preliminary tests that were required for entry. The recruiter got up and left the building during the test and two male recruiters asked Mary whether she wanted them to assist her with the test. She stated, "No thank you. This test is so easy that anyone who can't pass it shouldn't be a Marine."

In retrospect, Mary believes the offer to assist was also a test; Marines do not want cheaters amongst them. Also, she did not know at the time that there would be a battery of much more difficult tests to come after actual enlistment. During those tests there was definitely no offer of assistance and anyone caught cheating would have been prevented from enlisting.

Etta and the recruiter had set the meeting time in the evening, on a weeknight, after Etta arrived home from work. The family had moved once again, this time to a newly built apartment complex in a different section of southeast, just off the Suitland Parkway. It was the first time they had lived in an air conditioned unit.

Even though Mary did not hold out much hope, she awaited the recruiter's arrival with much anticipation. During the meeting Mary sat quietly, watching and listening to mother and recruiter discuss her future. The recruiter's efforts were stellar.

A young woman, approximately twenty-five years old from New Jersey, the recruiter had adorned dress blues in an effort to impress. She discussed the opportunities available through the Marine Corps, the testing methods used to assign careers, the procedures of "boot camp," the opportunities available for college and housing following active duty, etc.; still Etta did not acquiesce.

As a final attempt, the recruiter stated that she could arrange for a two year split enlistment term; Mary would officially have a four-year enlistment but would serve only two years on active duty and the last two years as an inactive Marine, receiving her discharge paperwork at the end of the second two-year period. Still, there was no acquiescing from Etta.

Finally, Mary stepped in to take charge of her life. She told her mother how uninterested she was in her current position in the typing pool. She told of all the dreams she had that were dying and how she really wanted to gain the self-discipline that the Marine Corps could provide.

Etta was unmoved by her daughter's plea, so Mary used her cut-card. "If you don't sign the papers I will go to South Carolina and get my father to sign them." Etta finally signed the papers.

As the recruiter left she offered Mary a small, reverent smile. She held a bit more respect for the young woman; she had originally thought her a weak, mousy little girl, but now took measure of her quiet undertones.

Back at work, everyone expressed good wishes for her future and sorrow over her departure. She knew for sure that most were sorry to see her go because she was carrying the majority of the workload. Even though she had received two promotions in record time, she felt very much used. Yet, she did not tell her coworkers that dissatisfaction with her job was the major reason she joined the military; there was no need to incense her coworkers.

❧ · | · ❦

Mary arrived at a military testing center in Baltimore, Maryland. It was an all day affair. There were hundreds of people there, recruits from all of the military branches were present.

Conversation centered around branch selections, entry dates, expectations and, in the case of the men, whether they had volunteered or had been drafted.

They had been indiscriminately grouped. The groups were led to different rooms for academic testing. After completing a test they were allowed to take a break, then the same group was escorted to a different room for a different test.

Bag lunches were provided and in the afternoon, Mary submitted to a medical exam. The doctor expressed some concern about the heart murmur which was revealed during the EKG. She informed him that she had been born with the heart murmur, that it had never caused her a problem and that doctors could not detect it with a stethoscope unless she had a chest cold at the time. She was afraid he was going to give her a medical rejection. He noted the heart murmur in her records, but indicated that it was not troublesome. She breathed a sigh of relief.

During the medical examination the doctor also expressed a slight concern over her weight. She was 5'6" tall and weighed 107 pounds. He stated that she was underweight by Marine Corps standards but mentioned no more about it and gave her a clean bill of health.

Her day of testing was over. She selected an entry date, April 4, 1971, and was transported home.

๛ · | · ๛

On Sunday, April 4, 1971, Mary was leaving the house with suitcase packed, heading off to Parris Island, South Carolina to become a United States Marine.

There was a taxi cab waiting for her outside of the apartment building. As she stepped through the door of the apartment into the building's hallway, she turned around to say goodbye to her mother and was taken aback when Etta kissed her on the forehead and told her to take care of herself.

It was the first time that Mary could remember seeing a look of loving tenderness in her mother's eyes and certainly the first time she remembered receiving a kiss from her mother. She was approaching her nineteenth birthday and this was the first time she had known her mother to show her any affection. It startled her.

As a child Mary had felt that her mother resented her presence, as though she had been a burden. Perhaps she wanted to be a loving mother but did not know how. She did not recognize the value of placing your arms around a child to hug them or of offering praise.

Mary's goal was to become self-sufficient so as to burden no one, especially not her mother. The job she held at HUD had not helped her accomplish that goal; she thought her Marine Corps enlistment would get her there.

Though Mary felt the sadness of having grown up without affection, she felt a greater sadness for her mother because she was unable to display warmth toward a human being that she brought into the world. It was no doubt a drawback of never having known her own mother.

❧ · | · ❧

There were lots of young people roaming the corridors of the airport in Savannah, Georgia. It did not escape Mary's attention that her last visit to Savannah, Georgia had been as a prospective student for Savannah State University. She felt no regrets.

Questioning conversation had revealed that this young man or that young woman, just like Mary, was waiting to be "collected" by the United States Marine Corps. In most instances, they paired-off into groups of three to five. With each new airplane arrival they scanned the baggage claim area to identify more future Marines.

Mary was there for approximately five hours but there were others who waited for a longer period of time. Finally, at approximately 10:00 p.m., a male Marine walked into the airport and announced that all Marine recruits should board the bus which was waiting outside. The luggage was loaded in the compartments below the bus and, exhausted from doing nothing for so long, they boarded the bus.

They were fatigued and happy to finally be headed to their destination. In short order, the bus entered the gates which, by use of a well lit sign, proclaimed a hearty welcome to Parris Island Marine Corps Training Base. They rode the bus for another hour or so, making many, many turns. There was some light conversation, speculating about what was ahead and relaying what few known facts there were. Everyone was apprehensive, yet excited.

Finally, the bus came to a halt. With startling intrusion a male drill instructor, complete with a "Smokey the Bandit" hat, boarded the bus and delivered instructions in a very loud and powerful voice that went something to the effect of: "ALL CHATTER STOPS NOW! IF YOU ARE CHEWING GUM, SWALLOW IT! IF YOU ARE SMOKING, PUT IT OUT! THERE IS A LINE OF YELLOW FOOTPRINTS ON THE GROUND OUTSIDE! WHEN I SAY GO ALL MALE RECRUITS WILL LINE UP ON A SET OF THOSE YELLOW FOOTPRINTS! GO!" The men scrambled to get through the aisle, off the bus and onto the footprints.

A group of male Marines unloaded all of the luggage from the bottom of the bus. After receiving another set of instructions while standing on the yellow footprints, which included the fact that they were all about to receive "special" haircuts, the group of mail recruits were instructed to pick up their luggage and enter the building. The Marines reloaded the remaining luggage and the female recruits were now headed to their final destination, with much fear in their hearts. The bus was silent.

After an additional half hour ride the bus stopped in front of a barracks building and two female Marines boarded the bus. They softly asked the ladies on board to gather their luggage and carry it into the building where there was a bagged meal waiting for them. The new recruits all breathed a sigh of relief. During the meal they were provided with a bit of information about what was expected of them and some of what they could expect.

They learned there were two training groups, each with a different set of drill instructors. The seniors were currently occupying one of the two upper squad bays on the second floor and the new recruits would occupy one of the two bays on the bottom level.

They also learned that the month of April traditionally did not produce a large number of recruits. They would be graduating in June, and a group large enough to occupy both squad bays on a single level was expected to arrive after they graduated from Basic Training, because the month of June traditionally produced the largest training group. Also, smokers would receive four smoke breaks per day, one following each meal and a final break just before bedtime; non-smokers could use that time to just relax or write letters, however, breaks were not promised – they could be taken away as punishment.

The training period was eight weeks long and there was a new training group every four weeks. A setback was a reassignment to the junior training group, so receiving a set-back was very undesirable as it meant an additional four weeks of training. A setback most often occurred after four weeks, at the start of the junior training group, if it were deemed that the recruit was not on par with training; but once there was a junior training group a setback could occur at any time for any violation. Most often it was the lack of advancement in physical training which caused a set-back. Mastering every aspect of the physical training was an absolute requirement.

On the first morning the recruits were awakened by the sound of professional cooking spoons being banged against metal trash can lids. It was their introduction to the female drill instructors. There were four of them; the senior drill instructor was Staff Sergeant Placken and Sergeant Brice was her second in command; the two junior drill instructors seemed to be in training. The drill instructors were stern and sometimes frightening, but not generally mean.

Over the course of the next eight weeks, the recruits would undergo a systematic transformation. Most prevalent for Mary was the introduction of daily exercise. She was in good physical condition but had never developed an interest in any type of athletics. They were required to pass a specific set of physical training assessments by the end of training.

Additionally, Mary was taken back to her day of testing in Baltimore – to the doctor's assessment that she was underweight. On that first full day, while the junior recruits were standing at attention at the end of their bunks, the drill instructors distributed their name tags. Some tags contained a red patch of color on the end, while others (only two) contained a yellow patch. Mary received a yellow patched name tag.

The servers in the mess hall (dining room) were trained to look for the color patches; those with yellow patches would receive extra portions and double desserts while those with red tags received smaller portions and were denied dessert. Mary had to gain at least three pounds before graduation. The women with color patches on their name tags were taken weekly to the medical facility where they could weigh themselves and gauge their progress.

Coincidentally, the other recruit with a yellow name tag was also named Mary. Considering the amount of daily exercise, it was difficult for the two Mary's to accomplish their weight goals.

On the second day their numbers swelled as approximately twenty recruits were setback from the senior training group. The new recruits were frightened by the large number of recruits who received a setback. The possibility that each of them could receive a setback later down the line became more real.

The recruits attended daily scheduled classes which included Marine Corps history, United States history, drill and special "finishing" classes. The finishing classes intrigued the ladies and they were often humored as they were taught the proper method for a woman to enter and exit a vehicle, makeup and nail polish application, and how to arch their eyebrows.

They learned to march on their own parade deck, a football sized field of smooth asphalt, taught by a male drill instructor, Staff Sergeant Manny Kool, who also doubled as the instructor for Marine Corps history. Mary would never forget his name; his moniker was almost as cool as he was.

On Sundays the recruits received the option of attending Catholic church services, Protestant services, or attending a "garden party" which consisted of hand manicuring the lawn (pulling weeds and picking up cigarette butts) surrounding the female barracks.

Mary was eighteen years old and until that point had only attended Baptist services. She took that opportunity to experience the Catholic faith. She learned to dip her fingers into "Holy" water, kneel and cross her body with her right hand before entering the pew to take a seat in the congregation. That is it. That is all she learned.

She had always been curious about the concept of the Pope, and had hoped to get the opportunity to ask questions of the priest, but it was not to be. They were escorted into the church for service and immediately following the service they were escorted back to the barracks.

Still, Mary has no understanding of the Catholic faith, which appears to worship God by way of the Pope instead of forming personal relationships with God or following the directives of the Bible. She wanted to know whether Catholics considered the Pope to be their path to God. Do Catholics believe they have to please the Pope in order to reach God? The answer continues to elude her but her curiosity no longer burns in that regard. She has since discovered how best for her to worship Him and feels no obligation to assign her beliefs to anyone else. To this day, even with a greater understanding of the Bible, her heart remains her primary connection to God.

The recruits were required to enter a gas chamber and, after the tear gas was released, properly don a gas mask inside the chamber or suffer the consequences. Successful completion of gas chamber training was required; it could cause a setback. After every recruit had experienced the gas chamber they were told to fall into marching formation. They were going to march back to the barracks. As they marched and sang cadence several Marines emerged from the wooded area along the side of the road and began throwing canisters of tear gas amongst them.

They scattered and while most were applying gas masks, a few tried to outrun the gas. Most memorable was the recruit who, having dropped her gas mask in the ensuing panic, took a gas mask from the hands of Staff Sergeant Placken, thereby leaving the senior drill instructor to suffer the effects of the gas. She became the most popular woman among the recruits, for shear nerve.

There were times when the rules were detrimental to some, such as the time the recruits with red hair had to have their hair dyed. The red hair was too much of a standout amongst a group being trained to operate as one.

There was one recruit who was unable to accept the temporary loss of her hair color. Even though she allowed her hair to be dyed, it created an identity crisis for her and she was sent home after she was unable to stop crying.

There were many incidents of recruits breaking down into tears and Mary was astounded by the number of women who were unable to accept the restrictive conditions for such a temporary period of time. Eight weeks (or twelve if they received a set-back) were all that was required; and, of course, in the case of the recruit with red hair, her then black hair would grow out red.

It was not unusual to be unable to fall asleep because of, or to be awakened by, the sound of crying somewhere within the barracks. To make matters worse there were usually several women trying to console the one afflicted, usually causing the sobbing to grow louder.

Upon waking one morning, the recruits learned that one of their fellow recruits had been sent home after she had left the barracks in the middle of the night and was discovered approaching the base exit in her pajamas.

Drill instructor school was located immediately behind the female training barracks. The ladies were required to rise each morning at 6:00 a.m. However, the drill instructors rose much earlier and delighted in singing cadence at top decibels as they marched pass the female training barracks at approximately 4:30 a.m. After the first week, the recruits complained to their drill instructors who reported back that they spoke to the drill instructors' trainers to no avail. The trainees hatched a scheme.

There were whispers throughout the squad bay.

"Wake up, it's almost time."

"Be quiet."

"Open all the windows as wide as you can."

"No, don't turn on the lights."

The distant sound of marching wafted through the windows. They were approaching. As the sound of drilling grew louder and closer, the drill instructor trainees began singing cadence.

The anxious women were instructed to stand pat, until the men were flush with the female barracks.

"Now!," someone shouted.

Marine Corps issued black oxford shoes were suddenly flying through windows, miraculously landing on the trainees and their instructors. Amid the chaos and yelps, the ladies could not contain their glee. They laughed and shouted promises of future attacks if the trainees did not permanently refrain from waking them.

Gentlemen as they were, the trainees did not re-launch the shoes. They gathered themselves and continued on, marching in silence. The ladies ran outside to quickly regain possession of their shoes and tried to get a few minutes more sleep before time to officially rise.

Bang! Bang! Bang! Again with the professional cooking spoons against metal trash can lids.

"I CAN'T BELIEVE MY MARINES WOULD ATTACK OTHER MARINES!," the tone in Staff Sergeant Placken's voice announced her anger. Sergeant Brice was standing beside her with a stern look on her face.

"THIS IS ABSOLUTELY UNACCEPTABLE!" Placken continued, "DO YOU HAVE ANY HOME TRAINING? IF NOT, I'll TEACH YOU MYSELF. IF YOU ATTACK THOSE DRILL INSTRUCTORS AGAIN I WILL SET YOU ALL BACK! UNDERSTOOD?"

"YES, STAFF SERGEANT PLACKEN," the recruits had been well trained. They knew the proper response.

"NOW GET DRESSED. BE READY TO MARCH TO BREAKFAST IN THREE MINUTES AND ADD AN EXTRA TEN MINUTES TO YOUR SMOKE BREAK AFTER BREAKFAST!"

The drill instructors walked out of the squad bay and the trainees smiled at each other. They realized that their drill instructors had to admonish them for what they had done, but the extra long smoke break signaled approval, perhaps because they had attacked the D.I. trainees as a squad; they worked as a team.

A couple of weeks later, the trainees returned to their barracks following afternoon classes to discover the entire first floor of the barracks covered with approximately eight inches of water.

A pipe had burst. The drill instructors manned the phones and a plumbing crew was dispatched to locate the source and make repairs.

Mary was leader of the squad bay floor detail and was concerned the water would damage the flooring if not removed immediately. She and her team jumped into action; they removed their socks and shoes, rolled up the pant legs of their utility uniforms and began scooping water with buckets and emptying the buckets outside or through the windows. The rest of the trainees joined in. They used anything they could find which would hold water.

After thirty minutes or so, a couple of trainee transport vehicles (referred to as cattle carts) arrived and a barrage of male recruits armed with mops and buckets took over. Mary estimated there were at least two hundred of them. The male and female recruits secretly exchanged smiles and winks. The male drill instructors directed the ladies to stand out of the way and in short order the male recruits had removed the last of the water. Later that night a rumor passed through the lower squad bay of the barracks, accusing the male drill instructors of having appropriated every mop and bucket in the PX.

As the recruits reached the mid-way point in the training schedule, the seniors were treated to a nice dinner at a restaurant in Savannah, Georgia. While they were at dinner a hand full of junior trainees, led by a junior drill instructor, short-sheeted all the beds in the senior's squad bay.

Short-sheeting is the process of removing one of the sheets and remaking the bed with a folded over sheet to make it appear as though there are actually two sheets on the bed.

When the seniors attempted to get into bed, their feet touched the folds and mayhem poured out of the upper squad bay while giggles spilled from the lower squad bay.

The next morning the juniors discovered their unit flag had been removed and put back upside down. They were delayed for breakfast as they scrambled to correct the flag.

Two days after the seniors graduated, Mary's squad was decreased by a number of recruits who had received a "setback" into the junior training group and her squad was now the senior group.

Approximately two weeks later the base received a new commander and there was a Change of Command ceremony. As Parris Island is strictly a training base, all recruits, male and female, were marched onto the main parade deck and all stood at attention during the ceremonial speeches. Shortly after the speeches began the skies opened up and the attendants were subjected to a flash Summer shower. The more rigorous physical training endured by the male Marines left them more vulnerable to the sudden change and a few of them passed out during the ceremony. Soon thereafter the ceremonies ended and the recruits were marched back to their respective barracks to dry out.

Toward the end of training the recruits were required to take a battery of tests for the purpose of obtaining MOS assignments (Military Occupational Specialty). They all sat for an initial set of academic tests. After the tests were scored some of them were called into a second set of tests, then some of those were called into a third set.

During the following week, the recruits' MOS assignments were provided. One by one the recruits were called into the office of one of the four drill instructors to receive notification of her assignment.

There was one college graduate among them. She was devastated when the testing procedures assigned her to cook school.

Sergeant Brice called Mary into her office. The drill instructor attempted to taunt her.

"You had the highest test scores and if you had enlisted with a four-year active duty contract you would have gone to air traffic control school, so you messed yourself up."

Why would I want to be an air traffic controller?, Mary thought, but knew better than to verbalize her thoughts.

"See, now you're going to electronics school in the California desert for a whole year."

Mary smiled. *California, yeah!*

Mary did not understand why Sergeant Brice thought she would have preferred to be an air traffic controller, but the drill instructor was wrong. Mary had no intention of increasing her enlistment period; at least not yet. In addition, she was quite pleased to irritate the drill instructor by showing no signs of frustration over her assignment. She was still unaware of what the Marine Corps experience would mean for her and viewed her MOS as a good career, but temporary if she did not enjoy the work.

Mary was quite pleased to receive an electronic school MOS. She was also quite pleased to be traveling to California, desert or no desert. Living in the desert and living on a Marine Corps base would definitely be new experiences and Mary viewed both as opportunities.

Graduation arrived and Mary realized that only thirty two of the original sixty seven in her training group would be graduating on time. Several recruits had received a setback, but approximately fifteen of them had fallen by the wayside and been sent home.

Mary silently hoped the setbacks would all graduate.

The day before graduation the trainees were returning from the mess hall when they encountered several civilians in the entrance foyer of their barracks. Several recruits ran to their parents and after hugs, kisses and greetings began introducing their newfound friends and fellow recruits to parents and siblings.

As she was greeting the parents of another Marine, Mary saw her own mother enter the barracks and was quite surprised. She offered a hug to her mother and expressed her surprise.

Etta replied, "I wanted to surprise you. I'm proud that you succeeded." Mary gave her mother a tour of the barracks area, introducing her mother to her friends and regaling her with stories of training.

The next day, the recruits' graduation ceremony began with the girls marching onto the parade deck where their guests were already seated.

Just as the ceremony was about to end, a designated representative of the graduating recruits stepped forward to make a presentation. The recruits presented Staff Sergeant Placken, who had received a new assignment, with an umbrella to represent the Change of Command ceremony, a mop to represent the burst pipe incident, and a scarf with which to cover her mouth and nose during the absence of a gas mask to represent the incident at the gas chamber. Everyone laughed; the new Marines were dismissed and they joined their family members.

Etta said to Mary, "It was quite impressive to watch you all march onto that field with your shoes gleaming in the sunlight. "

Later, at the barracks the new Marines hugged each other as each glowed with the acknowledgment of success, of becoming a member of such an elite group. Each was re-deposited back into the world with a brand new set of personal characteristics which would always be a great part of who she was.

The experience had become both an accomplishment and a beginning. They rejoiced with the silence of smiles that could not be removed.

Mary and Etta boarded a bus for Washington, DC. Etta insisted that her daughter wear her uniform all the way home.

Life Mark: USMC, 29 Palms, CA

Two weeks later, scheduled to report for duty on a Monday, Mary had decided to travel on Saturday to allow herself enough time to tour the base before the start of school. She landed at LAX airport in Los Angeles, California at approximately 6:00 pm. She was reminded of the day she reported for training and was left at the airport for hours. There were two more Marines from her recruit class who were also due to report for electronics school, Jennie and Andrea. Jennie had called Mary to coordinate their arrival, and had stated that she would call Andrea. She searched the faces of the travelers, looking for her fellow Marines, but the Los Angeles airport was much larger than the airport in Savannah.

Approximately twenty minutes later Mary and Jennie found each other. They debated how to proceed.

"I don't know if Andrea is going to show up at all," Jennie provided.

"What makes you say that?"

"I talked to her last week and she was really upset about attending electronics school. She said she didn't want to go."

"Yeah, but she wouldn't go AWOL (absent without leave). Did she say what time her flight would land?"

"No, she never mentioned anything about traveling to Twentynine Palms except that she didn't want to be in the desert, especially not for a whole year."

"Well, at least she didn't get cook school."

Jennie giggled, then added "She wanted to go to Alabama for administration."

"Why? I don't understand that."

"It's not so much the school as the location."

"Okay, but the school assignment is temporary. What's important is where you get stationed after school."

Jennie wrinkled her eyebrows then said, "Yeah, I guess you're right. Let's wait another hour just in case her flight hasn't landed yet."

"Okay, but we also need to locate transportation to Twentynine Palms. After we find Andrea, I think we should call El Toro and ask for a transport. What do you think?"

"Yeah, that's a plan."

8:00 p.m. arrived, then 8:30. The two women were exhausted and frustrated. They were discussing the pros and cons of calling El Toro to request a transport so late in the evening when they were approached by a young man.

"Hello, Ma'ams. Are you officers?"

The girls laughed. Jennie spoke first, "No, we are not officers. What made you ask that?"

"Well, you don't have any stripes on your uniforms."

Jennie replied, "That's because we are both Privates. We just finished boot camp."

"Oh. My name is Joey. Where are you stationed?"

"Twentynine Palms. My name is Jennie and this is Mary." Mary was content to stand on the sidelines and take in the conversation.

"That's my duty station too. I'm just home for the weekend. I can take you back to Twentynine Palms with me."

Mary was leery, "You just happened to be trolling the airport for Marines headed to Twentynine Palms?"

"No Ma'am, I was here to see my friend off. He got stationed at Quantico, in Virginia."

"Oh," Mary said.

"I'll be going back to base in the morning. You two can stay at my house, then we can go to the base in the morning."

Mary turned and addressed herself to Jennie, "I don't think this is a good idea. I think we should get an official transport."

"It doesn't matter how we get there, so long as we report in by tomorrow we're good."

"I'm not going home with him."

"Come on Mary, he's so cute but I don't want to go by myself."

Mary hesitated, but finally agreed. She liked Jennie but did not like this rash behavior.

The next morning they were awakened by Joey's parents, who had returned home to an unexpected situation and were not happy. Mary was first to receive the verbal attack, because she was camped out on the sofa in the couple's living room.

After yelling at Mary to get off his sofa and out of his house, Joey's father went off to find his son and continue his loud verbal assaults. He did not spare his son from an equally assaultive verbal attack and this time the assaults were assisted by an equally assaultive attack from the man's wife. The three of them were loudly expelled and placed on their way. Mary thought to herself, *I should not have listened to Jennie. I knew better than to stray from the official transport.*

They headed off to Twentynine Palms at about 8:30 a.m. Mary was quite surprised that the trip took better than six hours. At about 3:00 p.m. they arrived in front of the female barracks at Twentynine Palms.

The ladies had expected to see a squad bay-type barracks, such as those at Parris Island. Instead, they were housed in double units that shared a bathroom between the two units. Each unit contained a refrigerator and a sink. Mary later learned that they were actually being housed in quarters designated for single male officers. In truth, there were too few women stationed at the base to justify the appropriation of an entire barracks. Instead the women had been assigned to the top two rows of non-married male officer housing. While the officers were assigned a single unit, the enlisted women were assigned two per unit with twin beds. The female officers were assigned to alternate housing.

Mary felt free and definitely independent. When she and Jennie checked in at the barracks office they were greeted by Andrea, who had arrived the day before. She had landed at LAX in the early morning and had called El Toro to request transport. Mary snarled.

Mary had wanted time to explore the base before reporting to school Monday morning, but Saturday had been spent flying and roaming the airport, while most of Sunday had been spent traveling. She barely had time to unpack. Andrea lead them to the dining hall.

"So, Andrea, I hear you don't really want to attend electronics school," Mary struck up a conversation.

"No. I don't want to be in electronics school and I've devised a plan to get us out of it."

Jennie asked, "What's the plan?"

"I found out that the classes are structured by the week. We have classes Monday through Thursday, then we have to take an exam on Friday. If we flunk any week for two weeks in a row, we can't continue and they'll assign us another MOS. All we have to do is flunk out."

"I don't like the idea of deliberately labeling myself as a failure," Mary stated.

"I know but when we do well in the School of Administration it will outweigh the fact that we flunked out of electronics school."

Mary disagreed, "I still don't like it."

Andrea continued with her argument, "Besides, the first four weeks are all math classes. It will be easy to flunk them."

"Yeah, it will be easy." Jennie chimed in. "We just have to figure the answer to the math problem, then write down the wrong number, just one digit or one multiplier off."

"I still don't like it and I'm not sure I want to go to Administration school either."

"You can request whatever school you want. The scores that got us into electronics school were high enough to qualify for almost any other MOS. If we flunk out of electronics school, you could request air traffic control."

"I don't know why everyone thinks being an air traffic controller is so wonderful. I don't."

The three completed their meal then returned to the barracks. Andrea arranged to collect the other two the next morning and lead them to the school.

At 6:50 a.m. the following morning, the girls headed off toward the Electronic School. They had to walk briskly in order to be on time for the 7:00 a.m. student muster outside the barracks for the male students. The barracks were situated across the street from the school.

At the female barracks the day before, the girls had been informed by another female student that the Electronic School consisted of approximately 2500 students, of which thirteen were female, counting the three of them. They learned that the Marine Corps wanted to make a turnaround in its policies toward the traditional occupational specialties for females and the Electronics School was pressing to graduate more women.

There were several school administrators presiding over the morning muster and announcements were made with all students present. When announcements were complete they were called to attention and marched across the street to the classrooms.

A new class of approximately twenty students began every Monday. The classrooms were accessible from the outside of the building and arranged in order from Week One forward. The format was to take four days of lessons, pass the test on Friday, then move to the next classroom on the following Monday. The students enjoyed the fact that the tests were usually graded and scored, then class dismissed between 10:00 and 11:00 am on Fridays.

The structure provided an early start to the weekend. There were buses to Los Angeles and to San Bernardino for those who wanted to get off base for the weekend.

The first week of class covered basic mathematics. It was generally a review of elementary school math. Throughout the week Mary, Jennie and Andrea laughed at the level of math and how only an idiot could truly fail the test. They would have to concentrate on failing.

Mary was sent to the school's administrative office during that first week. She met with a Lieutenant who explained that a four year enlistment was required to attend Electronic School because of the length of time required to complete the school. With her current two year active duty enlistment, she would have less than a year left on her enlistment at the time of completion.

The Lieutenant requested that she extend her enlistment to a four year commitment. Mary recognized that it was a request, not a command, and carefully informed the Lieutenant that she did not want to make a decision about extending her enlistment until the end of the two year period. She left it as a viable possibility and was sent back to class.

On Friday the test scores were provided and only Andrea had managed to fail. Jennie had managed a poor score, but it was enough to pass. Mary received a perfect score. She announced to her friends, "There is no way I could fail such an easy test."

As the second week began Mary and Jennie moved to the second classroom together. Jennie expressed disappointment at moving forward to Week Two despite having performed so poorly on the prior week's exam. She vowed to do worse on the current week's test. Andrea was quite happy that this would be her last week. She needed to flunk the Week One class only once more in order to receive a new MOS assignment. It was quite clear by then that Andrea would flunk out and that Mary would not; but Jennie's immediate future was straddling the fence.

Both ladies wanted Jennie to side in their direction, neither wanted to proceed on her path alone. Mary realized that if Jennie flunked out she would once again be the only female amid a classroom of males. Even though she was less encumbered by her shyness than during her tenth grade year at Spingarn, she preferred to have a little female company.

The beginning of the third week saw the girls completely separated. Andrea was temporarily assigned to Base Administration as she awaited new orders for school. Jennie was looking forward to flunking Week Two again. Mary was looking forward to spending the next year getting acclimated to desert life; she thought, *"Better heat than cold."*

Mary could not understand the discord of the other two. She already knew that she would not be happy as an administrative worker. She had not been happy at HUD; and she suspected that neither of them would be happy in that career either, they needed more of a challenge. She had presented this viewpoint to the other two, but it fell upon deaf ears. She hoped they were not destroying an opportunity.

Becoming acclimated to Marine Corps life was not as easy as Mary had thought it would be. As recruits, the women had kept each other in line, always together and working as a team.

Twice, Mary caught herself walking during the evening bugle call, referred to as taps. The bugle played to alert the entire base that the flag was being lowered and if caught on the outside during taps or the morning reveille as the flag was being raised, Marines were supposed to stop, face the flag and, when in uniform, salute the flag. On both occasions Mary had caught herself and assumed the proper position before anyone else had the opportunity to correct her.

She had no such luck, however, when she passed the base General's vehicle without saluting the flag. The event occurred during her lunch break in the middle of a school day. She was on her way to the PX; she noticed the flag, but upon a cursory inspection did not see the General inside so she did not provide the proper salute. The limo came to a stop and the General emerged from the back seat.

"Marine, come back here and salute my flag."

"Yes sir." Mary turned and retraced her steps approximately twenty feet to where the General stood. She provided the General with a proper salute, stating "Sorry sir."

"Somehow I knew you would salute me, but now I want you to salute my flag on the front of my car."

Mary walked beyond the General to the front of the car and saluted the flag mounted on the car's front bumper. The flag was designed with the Marine Corps' burgundy color as the background with a single gold colored star in the center. It denoted a one-star, Brigadier General.

The General joined her at the front of the car, "Why did you walk by my car without saluting my flag?" His tone was stern, but not harsh.

"I'm sorry sir, I looked inside the vehicle and I didn't see you there so that's why I didn't salute."

"You have to salute the flag itself, whether there's anyone in the car or not."

"Yes sir. I will definitely remember from now on." Mary allowed a giggle to escape her.

"What are you giggling about?"

The giggle grew louder and she attempted to speak while giggling. "I'm sorry, sir. It's just that I've been out of boot camp for about a month and I'm already in trouble with the top man on the base."

The General smiled at her. "Well, just remember to salute the officers' flags whether or not they are in the car and you should be alright, Marine."

"Yes sir."

"You can go now."

"Thank you, sir." Mary provided a departing salute and returned to her original path, still smiling.

❦ · | · ❧

It was a Saturday morning. Mary was shopping at the PX. She was trying to decide between two dresses. One dress was beige with a rounded collar bearing hunter green trim around the collar and the short sleeves, the other was a deep rich blue sleeveless shift dress. Mary thought the beige dress spoke to sophistication while the blue dress was more sexy.   A deep voice from behind broke her attention.

"Hi, you must be new to the base?"

"Yes I am. How are you?"

"I'm fine. My name is Jaime."

"Mary."

"Are you a Marine or a dependent?"

"I'm a Marine."

"Enlisted or officer."

She giggled at the memory of Joey mistaking Jennie and her for officers. "I'm enlisted, what about you?"

"Also enlisted. There isn't a lot to do here on base, have you checked out the Enlisted Club yet?"

"No. I heard the drinks are really cheap, but I don't drink so why bother."

"There's also a dance floor and a billiards room. Why don't you let me escort you there tonight and if you don't like it you never have to go there again."

With a slight hunch of her shoulders she responded, "Okay."

"I'll pick you up at your barracks at eight o'clock."

"See you then."

They exchanged smiles. As Jaime walked away Mary turned back to the two dresses from which she was trying to choose. She jumped slightly as she felt someone behind her and a hand touch her waist. Next she heard a voice directed into her ear, "I like the blue one best."

She turned her head and smiled at Jaime. He had quietly returned to offer his assistance. After she acknowledged his choice with a slight nod of her head, he left once again.

At the E-Club that night, Jaime guided her through the club with ease. He stopped here and there to introduce her to some of his friends, then selected a table in the far corner of the room. Mary recognized a few of the women present as fellow Marines but more than that, there were looks of envy from women all around the club. She surmised that Jaime was sought after, while Jaime commented, "You make every woman in here want that dress."

She accepted the compliment with a simple, "Thank you," grateful that he did not mention she had chosen the dress he suggested.

"Sit tight," he said, "I'm going to get us some drinks."

"Don't worry," he continued after noticing the look of alarm on her face. "I remember that you don't drink alcohol."

Mary sat back and took in the scene. It was not what she had expected. There were plenty of people present but there was a distinct absence of the party-at-all-cost atmosphere exuded in the D.C. nightclubs she had been to. It was relaxing.

There was music being piped throughout but it was not blaring, allowing conversation at a near normal tone. She had noticed when they crossed the room, near the dance floor, that the music in that area was louder. She had also noticed that the back portion of the club contained pool tables. The open entrance to the back room was approximately twelve feet wide, allowing a limited view, but still creating a defined separation between the two rooms.

Jaime returned with two drinks and a bowl of pretzels. "You have a choice of cola or ginger ale."

"Either is fine."

He placed the ginger ale in front of her and the pretzels in the middle of the table, taking a seat across from her.

"So where are you from?" he asked.

"D.C. – and you?"

"Detroit."

"What do you do here on base?

"I'm with the artillery unit. Every day we ride out to the desert to practice shooting. We go so far out that it can't be heard back here on the main part of the base."

"Are you preparing to go to Vietnam?"

"No, I've already been and this is how I'll spend my time until I get out. Most of us are short-timers."

"I'm glad you made it back. I hear it's pretty bad over there."

"Yeah, but its done and over for me. I'm looking forward."

"Good. So will you be headed back to Detroit when you get out?"

"Yeah, probably. It's what I know. Don't you plan on returning to D.C. when you're done, or are you gonna become a lifer?"

"I haven't thought that far ahead. I just got here."

They spent the next couple of hours getting to know one another, then he walked her back to her barracks.

"Mary, I like being with you."

"Yeah, I enjoy your company too."

He kissed her on the cheek.

"Goodnight."

"Goodnight."

Over the next four months Jaime and Mary saw each other every day. Jaime was a take charge kind of guy and Mary was only too happy to defer to his demands upon their time. If he said, "We're going to visit my friend tonight; he and his wife live in town," she said, "Fine."

Their relationship was easy and both found it comforting. As a student, Mary's work day would end ahead of Jaime's. She would return to the barracks for a couple hours of study before Jaime arrived in the evenings. They would have their evening meal together, during which Jaime would let her know what they would be doing for the rest of the evening.

Jaime appreciated that they never argued, Mary usually deferred to his lead and she never whined if he did not plan anything extravagant or complain that he was not spending enough money on her.

Mary, on the other hand, appreciated that Jaime always planned their time together and they never had a bad "date." She was still young and had trouble expressing her thoughts so she also had an appreciation for the fact that her relationship with Jaime was so natural. They simply enjoyed each other's company.

At the end of one such evening, as they were standing in the parking lot outside of Mary's barracks, Jaime spoke.

"Mary, I'm coming up on the end of my enlistment. I'm going to get a place in town and we'll get married. I'll wait for you to finish your enlistment, then we can move to Detroit."

She was devastated. Although she enjoyed being with Jaime she had not given a single thought to marriage. She wanted the relationship to continue as it was. She had just embraced her freedom and independence. It felt great, but now she felt the whole world closing in on her.

"Jaime, I don't want to get married." She blurted out exactly what she was thinking.

"Mary, I love you. You can't do this to me."

"I like you Jaime, but why can't we just be together?"

The grimaced look on his face indicated that he was attempting to control himself.

Suddenly, he grabbed her arms just below her shoulders and shook her.

"How can you do this to me!," he screamed. He let go of her, again searching for control. Standing there trying to look anywhere but at her, his breathing was labored.

Mary stood absolutely still, having never before seen this type of behavior from him. She was almost in a state of shock. Understanding that any further blundered communication from her could push him over a dangerous edge, she wisely chose to say nothing more.

With his mind racing, Jaime lit a cigarette to assist his thought process. To Mary's surprise he moved in to kiss her. Suddenly, he held her tight then blew smoke into her mouth and down her throat. She began to struggle, unable to breath. After a short while, but what seemed an eternity to her, he let go of her. She stepped back, away from him, coughing and trying to breathe in fresh air. He stepped close enough to her to whisper into her ear, "That's how I'm going to kill you."

She held her head down as she began walking toward her room, grateful that he did not try to stop her and that men were not allowed beyond the parking lot. She spotted a male officer standing on the sidewalk in front of the first row of male officer housing. He was just standing there; watching. He said nothing and neither did she.

Safe inside her room, she was visibly shaking. As she mentally reviewed the incident she was mesmerized. She thought, *I've never been afraid of Jaime or even imagined that I could be. The threat to my life is confirmation that we're definitely not ready for marriage. I don't know him and he obviously doesn't know me. How could the fact that I'm not ready for marriage produce a threat on my life? I'm only nineteen; too young to get married. What do I do now?*

She slept uncomfortably that night, tossing, turning and waking to screams in her head. She had not been so afraid of anyone since Cory and she certainly did not relish the feeling.

As she dressed for school the next morning, she decided on a plan of action. Once in class, she asked to be excused to speak to someone in the school's administrative offices. Though she was asked what she wanted to talk about, she would not divulge to the instructor the nature of the problem.

Mary found herself seated in the office of the school's Master Gunnery Sergeant. Master Gunnery

Sergeant (level E-9), is the highest rank an enlisted person can attain and for that reason they automatically receive the nickname "Top."

Mary reported the events of the previous evening, explaining her fear and utter lack of knowledge to handle the situation. She explained that even though she liked Jaime she had just gotten away from her mother's control and she did not want to go right into marriage.

She further explained that she did not want Jaime to receive any punishment, but she was afraid to be with him any more.

The Master Gunnery Sergeant reassured her that nothing would happen to her or to Jaime and that the Marine Corps would ensure her safety. She was told to return to class and to relax, the situation would be taken care of and taken care of swiftly.

Jaime would be instructed not to approach her again and if he did so she was to immediately report that infraction to him. Top directed her to contact the base duty officer and request to speak to him if anything happened after school hours. The duty officer would know how to contact him at all times.

Miraculously, Mary never saw Jaime again. Later, she heard a rumor that Jaime had been released early and had returned to Detroit.

⚘ · | · ⚘

Mary was initially wary but there were no further threats upon her life. She became more cautious about creating relationships and learned to better express herself. She made it clear that she viewed marriage to be very far off into her distant future, at least not until she had rid her blood of the need for adventure. In truth, Mary thought all men viewed marriage as a method of obtaining either personal or sexual slaves, or both; but she did not vocalize that opinion. She simply stated that she did not think she would make a good wife, which was truthful.

Back at school, if her classmates learned of what happened they did not bring it up in conversation. Mary was able to continue with her life, having only the regret that Jaime had been so hurt and upset.

With her life back to normal, she developed a new personal routine which focused on socializing within a large group. She formed a socializing nucleus of fellow Marines who frequented the E-Club.

Shortly thereafter, Mary once again found herself in the office of the school's Master Gunnery Sergeant. This time she was there to request that the school allow the female Marines to skip the morning muster outside the male barracks because the muster concerned only the issues of the male barracks; nothing was ever discussed that concerned the women or the school itself.

Top explained that he did not have the authority to excuse anyone from the morning muster. Such authority could only come from the school's commander. He accompanied Mary to the commander's office, a Major, and went in first to address the Major. A couple of minutes later Top came out to get Mary and escort her into the Major's office.

"Good morning, sir," Mary greeted the Major following a proper salute.

"At ease Marine."

"Sir, I'm here to request that the female students be excused from the morning muster and that we be allowed to simply report to class on time."

"My Marines all march to class together every morning." His tone was stern and took Mary by surprise. She suspected his mind was closed, but she was there in his office and might as well give it a good try.

"Yes sir, but during the muster they discuss things that relate only to the male barracks, never anything that applies to the women. After hours of late night studying we could definitely use the extra half hour of sleep in the mornings."

"Marine, you will make my muster in the mornings. Do you hear me?" This time there was anger in his voice.

"Yes sir. I'm not challenging your authority -- I only came here to make a request."

"YOU - WILL - MAKE - MY - MORNING - MUSTER!" Mary was startled by his screaming. She was reminded of the male drill instructors at Parris Island.

"No, I'm not." Her voice was level and even toned. From the corner of her eye she caught a look of surprise from Top, who was standing approximately three feet to her right. Her response had surprised even her. She had not intended to defy the commander of the school; it just happened.

She felt he was wrong to address her with contempt. By that time she had become a Private First Class, just one rung up from the bottom of the ladder, but that did not mean she was to be abused.

She thought the Major's behavior was unbecoming a Marine – of any rank. Officers were leaders by virtue of their rank alone and it had never occurred to her that some officers would abuse their authority.

The Major hesitated, "If you don't make my muster you will receive office hours."

"Okay."

The Master Gunnery Sergeant walked to the door and opened it for her to leave. She provided the proper salute and once it had been returned, she turned to leave.

Back in the Master Gunnery Sergeant's office, he spoke to her. "Mary, why did you do that? What were you thinking?"

"I was thinking that he didn't have to talk to me like I was his dog. It wasn't what he said, but how he said it. I had respect for him when I walked into his office but I lost it by the time I left."

"Well, Mary, I advise you to think carefully about how you are going to proceed from here."

"Yes, sir. I will Top."

"Alright. Why don't you go on back to class now."

At the female barracks later that night, Mary set her alarm clock back by thirty minutes.

On the following morning Mary reported directly to school, having skipped the morning muster. That afternoon she was summoned from class and Top once again escorted her to the Major's office.

"Marine, you were absent from my muster this morning and I'm going to give you office hours."

"Okay, just don't give me restriction; you can take my money, but I'm not going to stand restriction."

The Major's anger was apparent. He was obviously insulted by the gall of this PFC.

"I'm giving you thirty days of restriction. You will be allowed to leave the barracks only to attend school and the mess hall. Additionally, every hour on the hour you will check in with the person on duty at your barracks to sign the restriction log. Do you understand!"

"Yes sir, but I'm not going to do it."

"Get out of my office."

She provided the necessary salute before leaving, but the Major simply looked up from the paper he was writing on and pointed toward the door.

A battle of wills had been set in motion.

Later that night at the barracks, the female Marine on duty knocked on Mary's door.

"Mary, I have a restriction log that you have to sign. You have to come to the duty office to sign it every hour on the hour until nine p.m., but you missed the first one so I've brought it to you."

"I know I am supposed to sign it, but I'm not going to."

"Mary, you have to sign this," there was alarm in her voice.

"No, I told the Major that I was not going to stand restriction and I'm not going to. If I want to leave the barracks I will, and I'm not going to sign that form whether I'm here or not."

"Are you sure you want to do this?"

"Yes, I don't deserve this."

The duty left to return to the office, obviously distressed over the course of events. She was concerned for what would happen to Mary.

A few days later, Mary was once again summoned to the Major's office. With the Top at her side, she once again received office hours resulting in another thirty days restriction for a total of sixty days restriction.

As she departed this time she did not offer the customary salute, remembering that the Major had showed no interest in her departing salute during their last encounter.

"Marine, aren't you going to salute me?"

Top had opened the door and she had turned to exit but had only taken one step. She turned, hesitated, then slowly lifted her arm to something close to a proper salute but not quite there, in obvious defiance. The Major's face contorted in disgust but he too lifted his arm to a near proper salute in dismissal.

Over the course of the next few months, Mary and the Major repeated the scene four more times. Mary received a total of 180 days of restriction. Their battle of wills had manifest into a challenge where each attempted to modify the behavior of the other. The Major used his authority to punish her, while Mary sought methods of snubbing his authority.

By the end of the sixth set of office hours, Mary left his office without offering any type of salute and when the Major asked if she was going to, she looked back over her shoulder and replied, "No."

Amazingly, the Major never threatened to remove her from the Electronics School, where she was an outstanding student, and Mary never thought twice about performing at a lower level or leaving the school. She was proud of her attendance at Electronics School and looked forward to becoming a graduate.

When Mary was next summoned to the school's administrative offices she met with a Captain who performed a Summary Judgment, the next level in the military justice system. The Captain acknowledged that restriction was not an effective method of punishment and he demoted her from Private First Class to Private, with the respective loss of pay.

Mary thanked him. She returned to class and resettled into her routine, still refusing to stand restriction.

Christmas was fast approaching as Mary was summoned to Top's office on the Monday beginning the last week of school before the Christmas Break.

"Mary, I think I may have come up with a way for you to get out from under all of that restriction."

"Great!"

"If you will just stand a little bit of restriction –

"Auggghhhh," it was like a muted growl.

"Wait a minute. Let me get it out."

"Okay, Top."

"Christmas is coming up. Don't you want to take leave and go home for Christmas?"

"Yes, but I don't have the money to get there."

"If I could arrange for you to take a military hop to get home that would help you, right?"

"Yes, a military hop doesn't cost anything."

"Okay, I'm going to call out to El Toro and see what hops are available. Meanwhile, I need you to stand restriction, starting tonight and sign the log."

"For how long, Top?"

"Mary, just stand it for five days and I think I can make the other 175 days go away."

"Okay, I can do five days."

As Mary returned to class she realized that she only agreed because it was Top who asked. Had the request come from the Major she would have flatly refused, probably stating that she did not care about getting home for Christmas. She accepted that she was being deliberately difficult when it came to the Major; and with that acknowledgement she decided to let go of the chip on her shoulder. If Top could end it all with such a small capitulation from her, she would let it end.

On Thursday, Top opened the door to Mary's classroom and indicated that she should step out of the classroom. On the other side of the closed door, Top handed her a document which authorized her military hop.

"I couldn't get you a hop into Andrews Air Force Base but I've placed you on a hop from El Toro to Norfolk, Virginia on Sunday Morning. Can you get home from there?"

"Yes, I can catch a bus into D.C."

"Good, are you standing the restriction?"

"Yes."

"Good. Keep going all the way through tomorrow night. I'll collect the restriction log from your barracks and take care of finalizing everything."

"Thanks Top. I appreciate you getting me out of this mess."

"You're welcome. Get back to class."

∾ · | · ✒

There were five of them, heading for the east coast; Mary to D.C., Karen and Bernard to his home in New York, Rick to Baltimore and Ben to Rocky Mount, North Carolina. On a Saturday evening, approximately 9:00 p.m., they arrived in Los Angeles. by way of the 29 Palms base bus. Ben, who had family in L.A., had arranged for transportation from L.A. to El Toro. The El Toro flight into Norfolk was scheduled to leave at 6:00 a.m. the next morning. The group, having been joined by Ben's cousin, Mark, who had agreed to be their driver and who was the same general age as the rest of the group, discussed whether to report directly to El Toro and wait or to have an L.A. adventure to kick off the Holidays.

During the course of the conversation it was learned that neither woman had ever been to an L.A. nightclub; matter settled. They would party in L.A., then report to El Toro for their hop.

They piled into Mark's sedan; it was a tight fit but they made it work. In the parking lot outside the nightclub, Mary and Karen decided to leave their military purses locked in the car, neither wanted to be bothered with them on the dance floor.

Inside the club, the group enjoyed the loud music and rhythmic bodies of young people having fun. At 2:00 a.m. the club closed and the group meandered through the throng of ex-partygoers to get to Mark's sedan. They were happy with their decision to begin the Holidays with a night on the town. Karen reached for and opened the back door.

"Hey, the car wasn't locked?," Mary asked.

Mary and Karen looked at each other then immediately began searching the back seat for their purses; gone. Mary remembered checking the back doors to ensure they were locked, but she could not remember whether she or anyone else had checked the front doors. She suspected a setup, but could not finger the culprit; and even if she could she doubted the culprit would fess up and return their belongings. Mary announced that all her money was in her purse, but Karen had placed her cash inside her bra.

The ladies faced an even bigger problem. Their military ID cards were required to take the flight out of El Toro. They decided not to call the police; they did not have enough time. Mark drove them directly to El Toro, where Mary and Karen would have to plead with the duty officer to produce new ID cards and he or she would have to do so in short order. The drive to El Toro was silent.

They pulled into El Toro at approximately 4:30 a.m. Luckily, the duty officer was very accommodating.

It took nearly the entire hour and a half available to complete the necessary paperwork and photographs for the two ID cards plus authorization and issuance of a pay advance for Mary.

The twin engine plane was a cargo flight. The cargo had been securely fastened in the center of the plane and the passengers strapped themselves into weaved cloth seating that lined the walls. They learned that the two male Marine flight stewards were from New Orleans, which was the layover location for the flight. On Monday morning the flight would take off from New Orleans and land in Norfolk in the afternoon.

When the 29 Palms Marines relayed the misfortune of their L.A. adventure to the two stewards they were promised a better time in New

Orleans and it was suggested that the ladies leave their purses locked in the base vault while they were treated to a night on the town. Mary was pleased; she was headed to yet another adventure.

The two flight stewards announced they were about to leave and began checking everyone's seat belts; then they approached the back of the plane and exited through the two open doors on either side of the plane. The plane was suddenly filled with the sound of twin engines and the two stewards returned through the doors they had exited and secured the latches on the doors.

Having to yell over the sound of the engines, Mary asked of one of the stewards, "Why did you get off the plane?"

"We had to start up the propellers."

Mary thought, *Oh my God, what have I gotten myself into?*

It took some doing to ignore the noise of the engines, but Mary and her cohorts managed to catch up on some much needed sleep. They had been in the air for hours and had made one touch down to refuel. They were once again in the air and on their way to New Orleans when the co-pilot announced that they were making an emergency landing.

Dusk was approaching as they disembarked. After landing they learned the nature of the emergency; the pilot had fallen ill. They also learned that they were grounded for the night, at Laughlin Air Force Base in Texas.

Par for the course, Mary thought. This vacation was destined to be eventful. Apparently the co-pilot had communicated with Laughlin AFB personnel prior to landing because the crew and passengers had already been assigned temporary quarters.

Mary and Karen were the only women aboard the flight, and they were not surprised to be assigned to room together. The ladies quickly showered and changed into civilian clothing then headed out of the dormitory-type barracks toward the dining hall, where the seven enlisted Marines had agreed to meet up to get something to eat and to formulate a plan to entertain themselves.

From the dining hall the group found its way to the E-Club and spent the rest of the evening providing well wishes for the pilot and making jokes about their night out in New Orleans.

The following morning, they spent a short amount of time in the air before landing in New Orleans where the two stewards were replaced by other Marines. The final leg of the hop was underway, New Orleans to Norfolk.

The anxious group of Marines was happy to be anticipating the final embarkation. They were sick of the loud engines and cloth seating.

Once they finally reached their destination they thanked the pilot and stewards for getting them to Norfolk safely and said their good-byes.

At the Norfolk bus station they made use of the public restrooms to change into civilian clothing.

They stayed together as Ben boarded the bus south to Rocky Mount. The others all boarded the same bus.

Mary would be the first of the remaining group to disembark as they arrived in D.C., then Rick in Baltimore, and Karen and Bernard would ride on to New York.

It was nightfall as the bus pulled into the station in D.C. Mary caught a cab home. She had called to let the family know that she was on her way home, but had not been able to approximate her arrival time.

She spent nearly two weeks relaxing and becoming re-accustomed to home as she regaled Alissa and her family with tales of Marine Corps life and desert sandstorms. Suddenly, the time to return to 29 Palms was approaching. Mary placed a call to Andrews Air Force Base to inquire about a return hop, but there were no flights scheduled into California.

Mary thought to contact her monitor. Every Marine has an assigned monitor to watch over their military career. She was due back on base in two days but she was unable to schedule a hop out of Andrews and did not have enough money to purchase a ticket aboard a commercial flight.

When she got through to her monitor at the Pentagon, she explained the futility of her situation. She had hoped that her monitor would have access to military flight information from other installations.

The monitor, a Gunnery Sergeant (E-7), arranged for a recruiter to drive to her home and transport her to his office at the Pentagon.

Mary detected a feeling of importance in the air as the monitor guided her through the halls of the Pentagon. Not only were there lots of high ranking officers from all branches, but their uniforms were top heavy with ribbons and medals.

"That was one of the Joint Chiefs," the monitor whispered as they passed an Admiral who was holding a conversation as he walked down the hall. It was impossible for Mary to tell whether he was talking to one of three male Navy men, the one male Marine, the female in civilian clothing, or whether his conversation was intended for all of them as the entourage worked to stay within hearing distance. She was awed by the scene.

Having reached the monitor's office, Mary sat on the other side of his desk as he made telephone calls and brandished official paperwork. Once or twice he left his office to gather information or paperwork, leaving her wondering where he had gone. She instinctively knew not to wander the halls of the Pentagon looking for him, so each time she sat patiently to await his return. When he was done he handed her a folder.

"Okay, Mary. This folder contains a ticket to board a commercial flight to Los Angeles. It also has the contact information for the transportation I've arranged for you from the airport to 29 Palms and an extended leave authorization so that you won't be AWOL. I was able to get you a reduced rate for the ticket, but it will be deducted from your future pay at a rate of $55.00 per paycheck until it is paid in full."

"Thank you."

"Is there anything else that you need?"

"No. You've taken good care of me. Thanks so much."

She was disappointed at having to pay for a commercial flight instead of utilizing the military's free air transport system, but immediately conceded that it was far better than the alternative, and she would end her vacation with a more pleasant excursion than it had begun.

Upon her return to 29 Palms Mary was taken aback by the surprise of her fellow Marines that she had actually been bold enough to call her monitor at the Pentagon. She replied that if they were not supposed to utilize the services of their monitors then they would not have been taught of their existence during training at Parris Island.

With the battle between her and the school's commander ended, Mary returned to school relaxed and with her mind at ease. Because of her extended vacation she began class on Wednesday and had to hustle to catch up to the rest of the class, but amazingly, she performed well on the test at the end of the week.

However, two months later she was forced to move to the class behind hers when she came down with a bout of strep throat and spent a week in bed. The Navy personnel at the base medical facility had provided medication and prescribed bed rest.

She recovered from the strep throat and returned to school, managing to immediately fit in with her new set of classmates. During the month of May, as her class was nearing the point of completion in the month of June, they learned they would attend an additional four week specialized training course.

Attendance would require they each receive a top secret clearance and the necessary investigations had already been requested. At the completion ceremony they learned they had each received the proper clearance and would move on as a class to a specialized training building on the following Monday.

On Monday morning, the class gathered at the gate of the fenced-in building and waited to gain entrance. The fence looked to Mary to be at least twelve feet high with barbed wire atop. They all dropped their jaws at the sign which warned of an electrified fence.

Mary had noticed the fenced-in building in its isolated location but had never given much thought to why it was fenced and had never guessed that the fence was electrified.

An instructor arrived and escorted the class into the building. He lead them to their classroom and again their jaws dropped. They were even more impressed with the very unusual security measures that had been applied inside the building.

Mary recognized the opportunity and immediately resolved to study harder than she had thus far.

Classes were taken far more seriously by the entire class and they completed the course without losing a single classmate. On the first day of the final week they learned they were being deployed as a class to Okinawa, Japan.

Mary panicked. She did not want to be in a foreign speaking country and had been hoping for orders near Washington, DC. Again, she called her monitor.

"My entire class has orders to Okinawa, Japan, but I don't want to go."

"Mary, Okinawa is a really nice duty station. Are you sure you don't want to go?"

"I'm certain, and I know they can't send a female outside of the United States without her permission."

"Okay. Have you thought about where you want to go?"

"Somewhere on the East Coast."

"Let's see, I have a billet for your MOS at Quantico, Virginia."

"Oh no, I heard they have a female Colonel there who is a terror. I don't want to be there."

The monitor giggled, "Alright, how about Cherry Point, North Carolina?"

"Well, I haven't heard anything about that duty station."

"Cherry Point is a small air station which is right next to Camp Lejeune."

"Okay." Mary was thinking that she might be able to take hops on a regular basis.

The truth, which she did not want to admit to her monitor, was that she had found the difference in East and West coast culture to be shocking.

During her time at 29 Palms she had ventured on many occasions to several California cities, including San Bernardino, Riverside, San Diego, Sacramento and Los Angeles. She had discovered a difference in basic views of the people in California versus the people in the Washington, DC Metropolitan area. She speculated that it was due to the major industries of the two regions, "Hollywood" versus "Federal government."

She thought, *Even though there is a great geographical separation, it was still the United States of America, and there should not be such a cultural separation.*

Mary did not think that one was more right than the other, it was just that she longed for the environment to which she had become accustomed and in which she felt comfortable. She did not want to feel even more out of place in a foreign country.

Her class expressed disappointment when they learned that she would not be going with them to Okinawa, but they were all headed into their military careers and everyone's spirit was high.

Life Mark: USMC, Cherry Point, NC

Mary had decided to take a two week vacation before reporting to Cherry Point. She needed to talk face-to-face with Alissa.

Arriving back at her mother's apartment, Etta greeted her harshly, "What have you done?"

"What do you mean?"

"The FBI sent investigators all around the neighborhood asking questions about you? What did you do?!"

"Nothing, Mama; I needed a top secret clearance so the FBI performed an investigation, that's all."

"You have a top secret clearance?"

"Yes."

"Oh," Etta relaxed. She was relieved to know that her daughter was not headed off to prison. Though she never said, Mary thought she was impressed that her daughter held a top secret clearance.

Mary had called Alissa from 29 Palms, California to say that she would be changing duty stations when Alissa informed her that Evette had died. Apparently, Evette had become one of the victims of a bad batch of mercury-tainted fish.

Mary had difficulty accepting Evette's death. Of the three of them, Evette had displayed the most promise for success. Mary had always admired her decisiveness. Evette held an uncanny ability to quickly identify a necessary objective, then just as quickly development a plan of implementation and place it into action.

Worse yet, Evette had left behind a husband and a baby girl, neither of whom Mary had met. She asked herself, "How could that happen?" Mary and Evette had not seen as much of each other since the three girls had been separated by different high schools, but she had kept in touch with Alissa and so had Evette. She realized that they had both allowed Alissa to be the glue.

Mary became conscious of the fact that her self-absorption was so complete that she had become selfish. She needed to reach out to others. She would begin by reconnecting and deepening her friendship with Alissa. She would also become a friend to her mother, a much more daunting task.

Seated in her friend's living room, Mary held Alissa's toddler, a girl, on her lap. "Alissa, I can't believe Evette is gone."

"I know. It was so sudden."

"I feel terrible about her husband having to raise their daughter all on his own."

"Girl, please. He couldn't wait to drop the baby off with Evette's mother."

"What!"

"He said he can't take care of her by himself."

"That's bunk. Millions of women take care of children on their own and there's no reason why men can't do it to."

"I know, but Mary, he didn't show much interest in the baby before Evette died. He likes to run the streets; even when Evette was pregnant he ran the streets. Evette had to call me a couple of times to borrow money for the baby's milk because when Ronnie did come home he would be flat broke."

"That's so sad. That child needs her father."

"Yep, that's what I like about Papa George, my father-in-law. His wife left him with four children to raise. He did it practically by himself, with just a little help from his sister."

"Where is that crazy husband of yours?"

"He's at work right now. He's a manager at McBride's department store, so he has to work a lot of overtime and weekends."

"I still remember the day you pulled me out of class at Spingarn and took me to the library so I could meet him."

Alissa giggled, "Yeah, he remembers that too. I had told him that if you didn't like him I would not be his girlfriend."

Both women laughed.

"I would only have given him thumbs down if he had been an egotistical jerk."

"Yeah, well, he didn't need to know that."

Again, they choked up in laughter.

"So, how do you like being in school and what are you studying?"

"Oh, I love Washington Tech. I'm studying computer science and Dr. Gennard, the president of the school, is fantastic. He created relationships with some of the largest businesses in the area. Many of the big organizations have made commitments to hire Washington Tech graduates. He makes sure his students find employment. After I graduate and get a job then my wonderful hubby will enroll in Washington Tech also."

"Oh! You two worked out a plan to support each other through college?"

"Yeah."

"That's great!"

"Do you plan on going to college when you get out of the Marines, or are you going to become a lifer?"

Mary's attempt at a giggle turned into something just shy of a snort, "I love being a Marine, but I am not lifer material."

"So, what are you going to do when you get out?"

"The Electronics School training should get me into a pretty good job. If it doesn't then I can use the G.I. bill to help pay for college."

"So you're still planning to get out at the end of your two-year enlistment?"

"Yep, I've discovered that I'm not very good at taking orders."

Alissa laughed. "Why? What's happening with the orders?"

"It's just that the ranking system assumes intelligence. You would be surprised at how many stupid people receive college degrees and enter the military as officers. Many of the guys who came home from Vietnam tell nightmares of officers arriving fresh from the states and trying to give orders that would get men killed. The officers were so full of themselves that they refused to consult with those who had been there for a time and knew the lay of the land, so to speak, simply because they held a lesser rank."

"That's crazy."

"Yeah, after a while those who had to do the fighting would ignore the commands of the green officers and just do what they knew had to be done. That is a greater sense of being a Marine than just a ranking system; and, of course, the stupid green officers received the credit for the decisions and successful missions of the very same enlisted personnel that they treated with contempt."

"Isn't that always how it happens?"

"Some officers concede to the sergeants' fighting knowledge on the battleground. When volunteers were needed for a mission they would first find out which officers were running the operation before they would step up. The guys also said that when there was an officer who understood what was happening on the battlefield, the men would support those officers against their superiors. "

"Yeah, I can see how you might want to ignore orders when your life is on the line. Mary, they won't send you into battle will they?"

"No, the Marines don't send women into battle. There are Navy and Army women manning medical stations and they sometimes get caught in the middle of battle, but those women probably have a larger concern over being raped than shot."

"Oh, my God! The women get raped!"

"There are hundreds of thousands of American men in a strange country, being shot at regularly, and their female counterparts are back here in the States. Yes, rape is a huge concern – for our women and the Vietnamese women too."

"Wow! So, is that why you didn't want to go to Okinawa?"

"No, I don't think rape is a problem in Okinawa. It's a non-war zone and I heard that a lot of American men marry Japanese women. They think all Japanese women are like geishas who only live to serve men."

"Mary, I think the Japanese culture raises women to cater to men."

"Even if that's true, let's see how many of those women are willing to give up their lives in servitude after they arrive in the States where the bras have already been burned in order to release them."

"Yeah, there will probably be a lot of divorces from those marriages."

"Either that or our American men will adjust to being with free-thinking, strong willed women who happen to be of Japanese descent."

"Or they'll apply for Japanese citizenship."

Again, the women broke into laughter.

They conversed for hours and hours on several occasions during Mary's vacation. They discussed everything from babies to politics. Throughout their entire friendship there had never been any shortage of conversation between them.

Mary spent so much time at Alissa's home that when she said she would be departing for her duty station on the following day the baby, who was once again in Mary's lap, began to cry. Mary and Alissa had not even realized that the child had been paying attention.

∾ · | · ∾

Cherry Point, North Carolina was a beautiful little air station situated next to Camp Lejeune. The two entrance gates were located only a few miles apart on the same road.

The female barracks for enlisted personnel at Cherry Point was a two-level dormitory-type structure. The rooms were designed to house four, with two sets of bunk beds in each room, but the number of women who lived on base allowed for two-to-a-room billeting. When Mary reported to the duty on call she was given her room assignment and directed to return to the barracks office after she placed her gear in her room.

As she entered the office area, she was directed to an office toward the back. She entered the office and stood at attention in front of the desk, "Good morning, Ma'am. I'm reporting as ordered."

"At ease."

There was a flicker of recognition. Mary noted the name tag on the desk. It read Master Sergeant Jansen. Oh! It was the very recruiter she had talked to during Armed Forces Day at Spingarn High School.

Mary spoke first, "Ma'am, do you remember me? I was in the Spingarn Girls Drill Team and you came to our school on Armed Forces Day?"

"Yes, I do remember you. Have a seat PFC." Mary had regained the stripe lost during her battle with the commander of the Electronics School.

"Thank you, Ma'am," she took a seat as directed.

"I actually received a phone call at home, warning me that you were on your way here and that you might be bringing trouble with you. So, I've had to spend my Sunday sitting here waiting for you to arrive."

"Ma'am, I can't imagine why you got such a call. It is true that I squared off against a Major while in school, but that's long since over and I'm moving forward with my Marine Corps career. I only have eight months left 'til the end of my enlistment."

"That's the other thing, I've been asked to inquire into the extension of your enlistment. It seems unfair that the Marine Corps should spend so much time and money educating you when your commitment is limited to only eight months."

"Ma'am, I'm confused. If the Marine Corps is so concerned that I'm such a troublemaker then why would they want me to extend my enlistment. It doesn't make sense to me."

"Yes, I suppose it is contradictory, but these are the things that I've been asked to talk to you about and to determine your intentions."

"Well, Ma'am, it is my pleasure to inform you that I am not looking for trouble --"

"Good, I'm glad to hear that."

"And whether or not I extend my enlistment will depend on how well these final eight months go for me. Thus far my career has consisted of boot camp and educational training. Cherry Point is my first actual duty station. I'm still waiting to know what being a real Marine feels like."

"Well if there is anything I can do to help you fit it, please let me know."

"I will."

"And if you have any problems of any kind please let me know that as well."

"Yes Ma'am, I will. Thank you."

"Well, that's all I wanted. You can return to your room and get unpacked."

Mary stood, "Thank you, Ma'am."

It was true that Mary was not looking for trouble, but she had not yet taken stock of the fact that evil sought after her.

As she was headed out of the barracks offices, she wondered if Master Sergeant Jansen was married to Master Gunnery Sergeant Jansen from the Electronics School. During their meeting at Spingarn High School then Gunnery Sergeant Jansen had stated that she was actually married to another Marine, but that they were not always able to receive assignments at the same duty station.

She thought that if they were married then it was more than likely he who had called his wife to say that she was on the way. He would have told her of all the events of the battle between her and the Major, more than just what was provided in the record. He would have given her the straight scoop and no doubt asked his wife to help protect her. Mary had felt a strong paternal instinct from Top and she was certain that he was looking out for her. He had protected her at 29 Palms and provided a protector for her at Cherry Point. God had provided the two Jansen angels. She was blessed.

Mary had almost completed unpacking when her new roommate entered. Her name was Jean. They exchanged cordialities and learned that both were from the Washington, DC Metropolitan area. Their parents' homes were less than three miles apart. It was a common bonding point and even though the two women never spent any time together outside of the room they shared, they held a mutual respect for one another.

Mary reported to her work location the following morning. She walked approximately eight city blocks from the barracks to her assigned unit.

Including Mary, there were eight people assigned to the unit. The only other female worked as an administrative assistant to the unit's supervisor, a Gunnery Sergeant, "Gunny."

The workday began at 7:00 a.m. and for the first few days Mary found herself the only one working during the first hour or so, as everyone else congregated around the unit's coffee pot. Before the end of her first week, Mary began drinking coffee. She did not enjoy it, the coffee was very strong, but she felt stupid to be the only one working.

She found her coworkers to be pleasant, but dismissive. They overlooked her. She found that if she did not initiate work assignments, she would be left to fend on her own.

She decided to perform a test. On the last day of the second week, she reported to work, at the coffee pot. At the end of the morning coffee break she took a seat at a work table toward the back of the unit. She did no work and said nothing to anyone. When the lunch break arrived she left on her own then returned on time to do and say nothing for the rest of the day. There were no objections from anyone; no directives, no instructions, no comments of any kind. She thought, *They want me to extend my enlistment for this? How am I supposed to grow?*

Mary began taking a more active role in the development of her career. When a coworker went on a field call she would offer to assist. If an objection or excuse was offered which would exclude her, she would ask, "How am I supposed to learn?"

When equipment was removed from the field and brought back to the unit for repair, she made a pest of herself until she was included in the process. She would even perform menial tasks such as cleaning the equipment or performing standardized equipment checks in order to learn more. At times it was like pulling teeth.

Mary learned that Virginia, the female administrative assistant, actually held the same

MOS as she and the other techs. Virginia was a short-timer; the end of her enlistment was nearing. She informed Mary that she had opted to work in the office; she preferred it to field work. Mary made no comment.

The unit had two pickup trucks. One was fairly new and gray in color, while the other was older, yellow and often broke down in transit. The shop techs called it the "Yellow Banana." Both trucks had manual transmissions.

Mary had learned to drive while in California. One of her fellow Marines taught her to drive his mustang sports car which had an automatic transmission. She had failed her first driving test in the town of 29 Palms, California when she failed to stop at a blind corner. Even though there was no stop sign posted she should have stopped because she was unable to determine whether all of the traffic routes were clear due to the shrubbery planted at the corners. During the second driving test, Mary stopped at *every* corner and received her first driver's license.

Virginia was assigned to teach Mary to drive a manual transmission truck. The gray truck was designated for the lessons. With Mary behind the wheel, Virginia directed them to a secluded area of the base where they would not encumber normal traffic. After an hour of just driving around to get used to using a clutch, Virginia directed Mary to make a three-point turn and go back in the direction they had just come. Mary pulled forward as she directed the wheel to the left, then backed up a little too far and suddenly the back tires of the truck were sitting in a ditch. The dirt in the ditch was soft; the wheels spun as Mary tried to move the truck forward.

After both women tried unsuccessfully to maneuver the truck from the ditch, Virginia used the truck's radio to call back to the unit and inform them of the current dilemma. The base motor pool was contacted and a truck was dispatched to assist them.

To Mary's surprise, the truck that arrived was large enough to tow an eighteen wheeler; it was extremely tall. The tale of two women Marines stuck in a ditch had amused the staff of the motor pool. There were not only two Marines in the cab of what they called a "tow" truck, but there were eight to ten more Marines mounted at various positions on the outside of the truck. They approached with yelping hoopla. "How in the world did you get stuck in a ditch?!" "Man, leave it to women!" "Do y'all want us to get y'all out of the ditch?!"

To the last question Virginia replied, "Why else would we have called you?"

Understandably, Virginia placed the blame where it belonged, explaining that Mary was learning to drive a stick shift, but both ladies received a couple more rounds of scathing horseplay before the men finally attached the tow gear then pulled the pickup back onto the road.

The ladies offered the appropriate gratitude then pulled away. They were smiling as they endured the last of the horseplay. "Don't forget to call us the next time you put it in a ditch!" "We're Marines, we rescue our women!"

With a little practice Mary learned to drive the manual pickup with ease. A week later, the unit held an exit party for Virginia. There was cake and coffee. During the party, Gunny told Mary that the gray pickup had been assigned to her and her alone. The men would all share the "Yellow Banana." She did not know what to make of the assignment, but thanked him.

On the following Monday morning, as Mary arrived at work, Gunny asked her if she would help out with some forms that needed to be typed up. She agreed. Gunny asked her to take a seat at Virginia's old desk.

He then explained that the four-page forms requesting promotion were due in two days. He further explained that because the forms were being fed into machines they had to be perfect. One typo in the document meant that it had to be discarded and redone. He provided her with a large stack of blank forms, as well as three sets of forms in which he had provided the handwritten responses.

Mary placed a form in the typewriter and began typing. It had been a while since she had typed anything, but it came back to her just like riding a bike. She found that she actually had to deliberately slow her speed because she had to toss two forms within the first five minutes. This was not going to be as easy as she had originally thought.

As the lunch hour approached she finally completed the three sets of forms without error and provided them to Gunny for review. She hoped there would be no changes because if so, she would have to redo the entire form.

To her dismay, Gunny handed her two more sets of forms to complete. She was about to retake her seat at Virginia's desk to begin working on the next form when Gunny made a request.

"Mary, would you be willing to stop by the PX to pick up a bag of chocolate chip cookies for me? My car needs some work and I'm going to do that over the lunch hour."

She hesitated, which prompted a further plea, "If you are willing to do this for me, you can leave now and return at the normal end of your lunch hour."

The extension added nearly thirty minutes to her lunch hour. She agreed.

"You're on shop business, so take your pickup truck."

In the afternoon, she set about typing the additional forms. Gunny was recommending the promotion of everyone in the shop; everyone except her. She was still new to the unit and did not hold a grudge. She expected that during the next round she would receive a promotion.

On the following day, she made a point to slip quietly away prior to the end of the morning coffee break to a work station. She was a technician, not a secretary, though she expected she might have to redo a set of forms or two if Gunny designated changes.

Toward the end of the workday Gunny informed her that she was needed in the administrative center to prepare promotion requests for other Marines from different units. Because the forms were due the next day, she might be required to work well into the evening but if she were willing to help out, he would excuse her from work the next day. It was not in her nature to refuse to assist when needed. He provided her with directions to the proper building and the name of the contact. She took *her* truck.

At the administrative center she was provided with forms that contained white out corrections and were, therefore, rejected by the equipment. Mary noted the irony of preparing documents that would utilize the equipment she was trained to repair. For some reason she could not manage to get away from clerical office work.

When she returned to the shop, Gunny solidified her position within the unit. He told her she was needed more in the front office than in the shop. He also informed her that he was willing to make extra concessions if she would assist him.

She was being manipulated with kindness and her arsenal held no weapons with which to fight it. She was outdone.

Her best effort at maintaining her MOS was to slip back into the workshop when one of her tech-mates would return with equipment in need of repair. She would assist in the examination and determination of the course of action, asking questions all the while.

When Mary had arrived at Cherry Point, the female Marines were already engaged in weekly training for the annual physical fitness examination. The requirements were different from those for male Marines, but the passing of the physical fitness exam was nonnegotiable for every Marine. Friday afternoons had been designated for PT (physical training) at the female barracks and no one was excused.

Students at 29 Palms had been excused from physical training in favor of their educational training. The honeymoon was over. Mary had only four weeks to prepare for the fitness exam. She reported to her barracks on Friday afternoons to gauge herself and train to accomplish the required number of sit ups, push ups and to accomplish the

600 yard run within the allotted time frame. (The requirements have since been changed to something a bit more stringent.)

Over the three week period she gradually improved her physical prowess to the point she felt comfortable enough to pass every phase of the exam. On the day of the annual examination, she proved she had accomplished the goal.

Following the physical exam, those women who had failed one or more phases were required to constantly train for re-examination while the others were given the option of participating in one of several sports on Friday afternoons. Mary chose the one indoor option, bowling. It was the first time she found a physical activity to be relaxing.

Bowling became the outlet for her frustration over the way she was being treated at the shop. She felt conflicted. She enjoyed the special treatment, yet she resented being deprived of her proper career. She bowled strike after strike.

Gunny had not requested an administrative assistant and when she asked about it he replied that his shop was already top heavy with techs.

She truly loved working with her hands and treasured the joy of rendering a nonworking piece of equipment once again viable.

It was like breathing life into a dead machine. Secretly, she compared the elation to the feeling a surgeon must experience after saving the life of a patient.

As the end of her enlistment approached, Mary continued to perform as the shop administrative assistant who wanted to get her hands into *their* work. She attained another stripe to become a Lance Corporal, but there was no doubt in her mind that she would not extend her enlistment. She certainly had no intention of fulfilling a clerical billet. She began making plans for her exit.

She inquired into the cumulative total of her pro and con marks (proficiency and conduct), the method which determines the type of discharge received. She hoped she did not have to extend her enlistment merely for the purpose of generating enough good pro and con marks to increase the average.

She happily discovered that she was on track to receive an honorable discharge. The only bad marks were issued at the time of the Summary Judgment. She had received good pro and con marks during each of the office hours, and great marks at every other turn. Her marks averaged well within the region to receive an honorable discharge. She was all set to enter the private work force.

Life Mark: A Fortune 500 Employer

In the latter portion of April, 1973, Mary stood in a long line at the Unemployment Office at Indiana Avenue in downtown Washington, DC. As a recently discharged member of the military, she was automatically eligible for unemployment. When she reached the front of the line, the representative directed her to the Veteran's office on the second floor.

She thought, *One well-placed sign could have helped avoid a huge waste of time.* She kept her comment to herself.

On the second floor there was a large sign over a door which announced: VETERAN'S AFFAIRS. Entering through the doorway she walked into an entirely different atmosphere from the despair which permeated the air on the lower level.

There was an air of socialization on this level, amongst both the government reps and the prospective recipients.

She quickly assessed the system used to gain assistance. The assessment also revealed that she was the only female present. She took a number then took a seat.

That too, was a different method than utilized on the lower level, where prospective recipients were forced to stand for the entire time they were waiting to receive assistance. Mary was grateful. It was a much more pleasurable environment.

As she waited to receive a designation for unemployment funds she struck up conversation with other veterans. In short order the inevitable question was asked.

"Which branch did you serve in?"

"Marines." The usual surprise was invoked.

"What made you choose the Marines?"

Mary's answer was always the same, "If you're going to join, you may as well join the best."

One might think that such a response would be met with disdain from members of other branches, but that was never Mary's experience. There was a healthy respect for someone who held high esteem for the branch to which they belong.

Soon she was called into a cubicle. There were three veteran representatives present; two of them were obviously displaced because one seated himself atop the far corner of the desk and the other atop a credenza.

She speculated that every female veteran was treated as a novelty. She had already accepted this shortcoming of the entire public, not just veterans.

The veteran seated behind the desk informed her that she was definitely eligible for unemployment but that she had to maintain a regular schedule of job hunting. He would actually arrange interviews for her.

"Do you have a copy of your DD-214 with you?"

"Yes."

She reached into her purse and removed the copy of her DD-214 which she had carefully folded over twice. She had not wanted to fold the original document. She unfolded the copy before handing it to him.

He spent a few minutes studying the document then opened a large book which measured approximately twelve inches by sixteen inches. The book contained a computer printout of available jobs. The veteran turned to a location of clerical positions and began reading job descriptions.

Mary's brow furrowed. She interrupted him, "Why are you trying to send me on interviews for a clerical position?"

"There are lots of secretarial positions open."

"Still, I would rather attend interviews that fit my MOS."

"Okay," he said sarcastically. He made it sound as though it would be a waste of her time.

"Thank you."

"Oh, here's one," he said. There was sarcasm in his voice and he glanced not at Mary, but at the veteran seated atop his credenza. He read aloud a job description that required the prospective employee to have a working knowledge of electronics and the ability to troubleshoot and repair electronic equipment.

"Yes," Mary said. "That fits my MOS."

He picked up the telephone and dialed the listed telephone number. The two visiting veterans snickered. He scheduled an interview then handed her a completed form which provided the date of the interview, company name, contact's name, address and telephone number.

"Meanwhile, I will begin your paperwork to receive unemployment benefits."

"Okay."

"Be sure to call me and let me know how the interview goes. I'll have to send you out on at least one interview per week, until you are either hired or your unemployment allotment runs out."

Mary rose, "Okay. Thank you."

The three veterans exchanged glances.

As she exited the building Mary was filled with an air of indignation. She was upset over the general tone of the meeting. She was not sure whether the men were disdainful because her MOS was traditionally held by men or whether they just did not want women in the military. Either way, she was not going to give in to the archaic prejudices of those three men or any others.

She steamed as she thought about how he had tried to ignore her MOS, opting instead to turn her into a secretary, again. There was nothing wrong with being a secretary, but her electronics option could prove more lucrative.

∼ · | · ∼

Mary presented well in the interview. She was careful to speak with perfect diction and to eliminate the use of substandard English.

When asked if she had any questions she replied, "You said that this side of the engineering force works with the smaller personal computers, but what about the other side?"

"They work on the larger computers, those that require specialized rooms with air conditioning below the floors. The rooms often have banks and banks of tape and disc equipment. They are usually the computers that run big companies."

"Well, I want to work on the big stuff."

"Hold on a minute, I'll talk to my counterpart on the other side."

He left her seated in his office, returning a few minutes later to guide her to an office on the opposite side of the same floor. He introduced her to the manager of that department, handed her résumé to him and made his departure.

In the second interview, Mary expressed an interest in building an electronics career in that department. She realized she was being quite bold, but she felt she was in a battle. If she did not stand up for herself she might be treated unjustly.

The manager agreed that she was qualified. He expressed a desire to hire her and offered her a position in his department. She was delighted. They agreed on a starting salary and a start date, then shook hands.

As he escorted her towards the door he said, "Congratulations, you are now an Associate Customer Engineer for IBC. Is there anything you want to ask me?"

"Well, yes. What does IBC stand for?

He laughed. "It stands for International Business Computers."

"Oh. Okay."

After the interview, Mary arrived back at her mother's apartment before the end of what would be a normal workday. She could not wait to make the telephone call.

"Hello."

"Hi. This is Mary. How are you?"

"I'm fine."

"I'm calling to let you know how the interview went at IBC."

"Oh, yeah! How did it go?"

"Pretty well, I got the job."

"Really?"

"Really."

"Did you get a descent salary?"

Mary told him how much money she would be making.

"That's a good salary."

"I think so too."

She could practically feel him searching for what to say next. "Okay, well you got hired so quickly that you won't even need the unemployment."

"No, I won't."

"Congratulations. If there is anything I can do for you in the future, please let me know."

"Thank you. I will."

"Good-bye."

"Bye."

Hearing the disbelief in his voice was just as satisfying to Mary as actually receiving the position. She smiled to herself.

ᴥ · | · ᴥ

New York, New York; she caught a cab from Port Authority to the Manhattan hotel. She asked the cab driver about the building across the street from the hotel. "It looks important," she stated.

"Lady, that's Madison Square Garden, everybody knows that building."

"Well now I do too."

Nightfall had already covered the city. She approached the registration desk.

"Hi. I have a registration made by my company, IBC."

"Yes, the IBC employees have been set up two to a room and your roommate has already arrived." The clerk handed over a key which indicated the room number on the key chain.

"Thank you."

As she entered the room, she could hear the shower running in the bathroom. There was an open suitcase on one of the beds and she placed her own on the other. She had already begun placing items from her suitcase into the drawers of the dresser closest to her bed when the door to the bathroom opened. In the doorway of the bathroom stood a man with a towel wrapped around his midsection.

"Uh-oh," she said.

"Are you here for IBC training class?"

"Yes, and you?"

"Yes."

"Well, there has obviously been a mix up somewhere. I'll go back down to the desk and see if I can get this straightened out."

"Well, give me a second to get dressed. I'll go down with you."

"Okay." She repacked her bags as her "roommate" gathered some clothing and went back into the bathroom to get dressed.

At the registration desk, the clerk called for a manager to assist with the resolution of the issue. The manager explained that IBC made her reservation in the name of Mister. "See," he said to Mary, showing her the typed reservation request. Mary recognized the problem immediately.

"Actually they used my first two initials, M and R, which stand for Mary Ruth."

"Oh. We didn't know Miss."

"It's not your fault. I'll have to find out who makes the reservations and request that they use my full name from now on."

"Yes, that will help."

"I'm sorry for the confusion. Do you have another room available?"

"Yes Ma'am. I can place you in a single room."

"Thank you."

The two IBC employees returned to the elevator. Mary's new room was located two floors above the other.

Mary thought, *"Well, for now I have a room to myself, but if there is another female in the class I may have to accept yet another reassignment to share a room with her."*

She resolved to enjoy her night alone, but chose not to totally unpack just yet.

The next morning Mary reported to the location of training in the office building above Madison Square Garden. She was relieved to discover that she was the only female in the class. It was a turnaround from her days in mechanical drawing class at Spingarn and electronics training at 29 Palms. It was not that she had developed an appreciation for being the only female in class; instead, it meant she would not have to share a hotel room.

The training period was three months; there were twelve IBC trainees from Washington, DC, Delaware, New Jersey and New York State. They were all there to learn the basics of providing maintenance and repair for IBC computers and peripheral equipment. It was the launching of twelve new careers.

Three months later, all twelve new employees were notified of successful completion of training and congratulated as they were announced as official IBC employees.

☙ · | · ❧

While in New York, IBC had covered the cost of the hotel directly and each student received a stipend of $24 per day for meals. Occasionally Mary would withdraw money from her bank account due to splurging on meals, traveling home for the weekend, or shopping for clothes, but she allowed the majority of her salary to accrue in her bank account.

She planned to purchase a vehicle the very week she returned to Washington, DC. She had searched the newspaper ads and decided to look at a Camaro being advertised at a used car lot. Her plan was to pay cash for the vehicle, thereby avoiding a car note. She asked her mother to drive her there, but on that day they were joined by two of Mary's older cousins, Fala and Chase. Mary wanted very much to purchase the Camaro but her mother expressed fears over her daughter being behind the wheel of a fast sports car. Mary came to realize that her mother had enlisted the assistance of her two cousins to help talk her out of purchasing the Camaro and steer her towards the purchase of a brand new economy car instead. At the end of the day Mary found herself at a Datsun dealership, completing the paperwork to purchase a brand new Datsun 610 with five miles on the odometer and a car note which indebted her to monthly payments for the next three years.

Okay, is everybody happy? No, Mary was not, but she was pleased that she had made her mother happy. For her next accomplishment, Mary set her mind to getting her own apartment. She thought, *I can't allow myself to be manipulated anymore, not by anyone.*

❦ · | · ❧

Back at IBC in Washington, DC, Mary learned that the group to which she was assigned included IBC's own on-site demonstration center and much of the surrounding downtown area.   Initially, she received first responsibility for five computer centers, but there were multiple levels of backup should she need help. She had a regular maintenance schedule to maintain.   Additionally, she was required to respond when dispatch contacted her with a specific call for assistance.

It was the lunch hour. She was shopping in a Connecticut Avenue boutique.   Her beeper sounded its alarm. Mary asked the clerk behind the desk for permission to use the store's telephone.

"Hi. This is Mary. You paged me?"

"Yes, Mary. We had a call from your account on 20th street. The printer stopped working."

"Okay, I'm on my way."

As Mary returned the telephone to the store clerk, explaining that she would return another time to complete her shopping, another patron approached her in a secretive manner.

The woman whispered, "Are you an undercover agent?"

Mary smiled and replied, "No, I work for IBC. One of my accounts needs my help to get their equipment running."

"Oh, I thought you were off on a secret mission."

"No, I'm afraid my heart couldn't take that type of excitement." The two women smiled at one another then Mary left the store.

Arriving a few minutes later, she walked into the computer room carrying her tool bag which was designed to look like a briefcase. She quickly spotted the printer, an intimidating piece of equipment which stood approximately 4 ½ feet tall, 4 feet wide and 3 feet in depth. She had shut off the printer's power and had just opened the side of the equipment and made an observation when a man approached her.

"Hey, what are you doing?"

"Hi. My name is Mary. I'm from IBC. I'm here to fix your printer."

"Oh, no you're not. I manage this computer center and I don't want any women working on my equipment."

"Well, if you don't want me to work on it I won't."

"Good, cause I don't want you working on it.
"

"Could I use the phone to call my manager?"

"Yes, it's over there, tell IBC to send me a man," he pointed toward a telephone sitting on a desk near the entrance to the computer center.

"Hi Ralph. This is Mary. I'm at the client's account to fix the printer, but the manager of the computer center says he doesn't want a woman working on his equipment so you'll have to send someone else to fix it."

"Don't worry about it Mary. Just pack up and come on back to the office."

"Okay."

Three days later Mary was summoned to Ralph's office.

"Mary, did you get a look at what was happening with the printer in that account where you weren't allowed to work on it?"

"Yes, it looked like a fuse was blown. I had an extra in my bag but I wasn't allowed to make the replacement."

"I suppose it is possible that there was a problem beyond the fuse?"

"Sure, there could be something specifically causing the fuse to break the circuit but I wouldn't assume that. I would replace the fuse then wait to see if the circuit tripped within a short period of time. Was there a larger problem? Who did you send to fix it?"

"I sent you to fix it."

"But didn't you send someone else after I left?"

"No. I sent a trained IBC engineer and she wasn't allowed to do her work. So I want you to go there now and fix that printer."

Mary smiled, "Okay."

Approximately twenty minutes later, Mary reentered the computer center from which she had been ejected and was met by the same manager. This time he was frantic.

"I haven't been able to print anything for three days!"

"I'm going to take a look at it right now."

Again, Mary powered down the printer and opened it from the side. This time she pulled the blown fuse and replaced it with a good one from her tool bag. She powered up the printer and ran a quick test, then turned to the manager.

"Everything should be alright now. If you want to run a print job I'll stick around to make sure it's running properly."

As the manager positioned himself at the computer's console, Mary prepared her incident report. Incident reports contained the information regarding the repair and the amount of time spent making the repair. It was the main source used by IBC for billing purposes.

As they heard the click clack noise of the printer, both she and the manager positioned themselves in front of the printer as they watched the paper being drawn through the machine and ink deposited onto the page at super speed.

The manager spoke first, "Thank you, Mary."

"You're quite welcome."

She left the computer center with still no understanding of why some people had such a problem with women occupying a position in the field of technology, but assured that she had helped create one convert.

She also thought about how wise Ralph had been. She vowed to do a good job for him.

Two weeks later she learned that Ralph had been transferred to another IBC office. She assumed it had something to do with the 3-day repair situation, but was unable to glean the reason through the use of the office gossip mill.

She had queried -- not the engineering work force that treated her with distrust, but -- the clerical office staff. However, she was still too new within the company to have earned the necessary trusts. Mary knew from experience that nothing could happen in a company without the production of paperwork. The clerical staff is usually more privy to the background events of a company than most of the executive staff.

Ralph's transfer left her with a bitter taste. It appeared that not only could there be a detriment for women in this field, but it could be detrimental for the men who assisted them. She had to be cautious.

She wondered just how much time was spent by other IBC employees concerning themselves with her career. Surely, they had better things to do.

Meanwhile, life continued forward as Mary moved into her first apartment. It was a garden apartment community in Suitland, Maryland, a suburb of D.C.

∼ · | · ∼

"Mary, how do you spend your personal time?"

"It's sad really. I go to work, I go home, then I wake up in the morning and do it all over again."

"Yeah, that is sad. Would you like to catch a movie with me Friday night?"

"Sure."

"Okay. Give me your address and I'll pick you up."

He was a coworker, Herb. She had never before dated a coworker and was unaware of the dangers. She was also still quite naïve.

The movie was *The Exorcist*. Mary watched much of the movie from behind the palms of her hands. Only on the way to the movie had she warned Herb that she did not normally watch horror flicks. It did not help that the movie was rumored to be based on a true story which occurred in Washington, DC. Still, she enjoyed Herb's company. They had dinner and a rousing conversation afterward. He was easy to talk to.

They began to see each other fairly regularly, though they did not show interest in one another in the presence of other coworkers. Their telephone conversations were infrequent, but when he did call her they often fought to end the conversations which flowed with ease.

Herb liked to surprise her with the plans he made to spend time with her. Most memorable for her was the Sunday he called and suggested a picnic.

"Hey, what are you doing?"

"Nothing. Why?"

"How about a picnic?"

"That sounds good. I could fry up some chicken and make potato salad."

"No, no, don't worry about cooking. We'll stop and pick up some food."

"Oh, great!"

"So, I'll pick you up in thirty minutes. Okay?"

"Okay. See you then."

"Bye."

"Bye."

Mary had been in a few relationships since Jaime, but none of them had felt as comfortable to her as she had felt in her relationship with Jaime, before he threatened her life anyway. There had not been anyone with whom she had considered spending her future, until Herb. He was always upbeat and positive. He lifted her spirits.

Again, he was in a very happy mood when he arrived. They rode in his car, an expensive sedan which afforded more comfort than her Datsun 610. He began driving and navigated his way onto the 495 Beltway. Soon, they were on Interstate 95 headed north toward Baltimore. Mary finally thought to ask.

"Herb, where is this picnic location?"

"Pennsylvania."

"What! We're going all the way to Pennsylvania for a picnic?"

"Yes."

Mary giggled. "Okay."

As they were nearing the Maryland/ Delaware border, it began to rain. They developed a rain contingency plan; if it were raining when they reached their destination in Pennsylvania; they would have their picnic inside the car.

When they reached Pennsylvania they found a fast food restaurant and Herb purchased the picnic lunch of chicken and sides. The rain stopped just as they entered the park. The passing rain had left daylight in its wake, but not much sunlight. It felt closer to dusk than it actually was. Herb unloaded the blankets he brought to place on the grass, but they decided to place the blankets over a picnic table's bench seat instead. There were families around with small children and they enjoyed watching the children play as they ate. It was peaceful.

The return trip to Maryland was dreamlike. Mary found herself thinking that she might have found a man she could actually live with.

As they grew closer Mary found it difficult to eliminate signs of their relationship while at work. Still, she had to. It would not have been good to provide fodder for the gender mad undertones of the office, which would have been fanning the flames.

One Saturday morning, Mary wanted to talk to Herb. She realized that she had never asked for his telephone number. She had allowed him to guide the entire relationship, but at that moment she craved his company. She contacted the IBC dispatcher.

"Hey, I need to talk to Herb. Can you give me his home number?"

"Are you sure you want to do that?"

"Of course I'm sure."

"Okay, here's his number."

"Thank you."

Mary dialed the telephone number. A woman answered, she never gave thought to who the woman might be.

"Hello. Can I speak to Herb?"

"Who is this?!"

Mary stumbled. Why was this woman yelling at her?

"Who is this?"

"This is Herb's wife, that's who it is! -- and I want to know why you're calling my house asking for my husband!"

Again she stumbled. This time the silent pause was quite notable.

"I work with Herb and I was calling to ask him a question about a piece of equipment."

"No you weren't! Don't lie to me and don't call my house again!" Click.

Mary thought, *Oh my God! How stupid have I been? I never asked if he was married. I just assumed that he was single because he was acting as though he was single. He spoke of our relationship in future terms.*

He did not seem like the kind of person who would deceive her, but what is a deceiver like? She felt stupid. She noted her own part in the infringement -- she had not asked for his telephone number nor thought about why they never spent time at his home. She had been proud of the fact that she wasn't crowding him. Had she deliberately closed her eyes?

In retrospect, she had also ignored the concern from the dispatcher. Why had the dispatcher asked if Mary was sure she wanted to call him at home? What else was known to everyone except her? Had something like that happened before?

Why had he done that? Why had he allowed evil to use him? She did not understand. He had presented himself to her as an available mate when he actually was not. He had risked his marriage. She did not want to see any marriage fail, let alone take part in its destruction. Still, she refused to carry the weight – it was all his.

What if he wanted to leave his wife and spend his time with her? Oh no, nix that thought. How could she trust him? If he cheated on his wife, he would cheat on her too. What she had thought was a great relationship had amounted to a complete hoax and it was now over.

They were coworkers; she would have to be civil to him and learn to control feelings of anger and disgust. She realized that she had been naïve but being naïve trumped the fact that he was a jackass.

Of the two positions, naivety and jackass, hers was the position of innocence; still, she would take future precautions to ensure that it never happened again. She found herself fighting to believe that not all men were jackasses. Could there be one good one in the bunch? Her hopes were very low.

When she returned to work she learned that Herb had managed to get himself moved to another department. She was grateful; she rarely saw him.

Mary proceeded into her career at IBC under the absolute realization that she had no allies within the company. Not only was she fighting alone, but everyone was a potential enemy.

When she had reason to frequent the administrative offices, the clerical staff made sly insinuations indicating they were privy to the most private parts of her life by virtue of the files they maintained plus anything tossed into the gossip mill, truthful or not. Apparently, Herb's wife had made a complaint and now everyone thought they knew who she was. Anytime she had to enter the world of administration, she steeled herself for what might come next.

A few months later, Mary was scheduled for further training, this time for two weeks in Chicago, Illinois. She was building a reputation as a good technician.

It was the month of May and Mary had falsely assumed that Chicago spring weather was similar to spring weather in Washington, DC. Her lightweight coat was insufficient to ward of the icy Chicago winds.

The hotel and the training were both in the area of The Loop. It was especially cold at the end of the training day, after the sun had gone down. When she returned to her hotel room from the training location one block away, it would take at least an hour before she warmed up again. Two weeks later, she returned to the downtown office with brand new knowledge and another bout with strep throat.

Mary was proud when one of her coworkers asked her to take a call from one of his accounts. She felt she was being accepted. As she approached the building she noticed people standing out on the sidewalk holding signs. Oh yeah, she remembered seeing something on the news about the DC teachers calling a strike. The account was an education association. Well, she was not there to take any of their jobs. She entered the building and found the computer room. The task was an easy one and twenty minutes later she was exiting the building to return to her group's headquarters. A man approached her on the sidewalk.

"Hey, why did you cross our picket line?"

"Oh, I'm just with IBC. I had to fix a piece of equipment."

"Yeah, but you still should not have crossed our picket line."

"I'm sorry, but my company has a contract that has to be fulfilled."

"Okay, we'll let you go this time but please don't do that again."

"Okay."

With that exit conversation she realized that she had not been placed in a position of trust after all. She actually had been sent to cross the picket line because no one else in the department was willing. They had not informed her. It was a setup. Maybe they thought she would be physically attacked, or at the least, that she would be denied access. In that event someone would no doubt have contacted management to point out her failure. Her anger rose, but she put it in check.

Mary moved forward in her career. Alissa was her sounding board, but she did not dump everything onto her friends shoulders. Alissa had her hands full as she juggled the tasks of wife, mother and career.

Because Mary did not have a family she had been designated to perform weekend duty over the Thanksgiving Holiday. She thought, *Just because I don't have children doesn't mean I don't have a family.* But, in an effort to get along, she did not argue. She was not required to be at a given location, only to accept emergency calls from dispatch.

"Mary, you're needed at the Richard's Bank main office on "F" Street. They have a disc that isn't working."

"Okay, I'm on my way. I'll call you if there's trouble."

It was Mark's main account. Mark was a very sweet man who convinced Mary to start using her seatbelt after he lost a son in a car accident. Mark thought his son would still be alive had he been wearing his seatbelt, but he was not bitter over the loss of his son. Instead, he honored his son by saving the lives of others. Mark was the type of person who exemplified God's Word without beating you over the head with it.

Mary arrived on site and had to be buzzed into the building. It was Black Friday and even though the bank was closed, its very popular credit card business was operating all over the area. She met with the onsite computer manager who guided her to the location of the single disc in the bank of thirty discs, two per machine, that was not working. The information contained on that disc was therefore unavailable to the system as it received requests for verification from retailers.

"I'll have to take the disc offline as I troubleshoot the problem and that information will definitely be unavailable to you while I troubleshoot the problem."

"How long?"

"There is no way to tell right now. I have to locate the problem before I can estimate the repair time."

"Well, I can live with it as long as you don't take down the entire system."

"No, don't worry. There is a switch in the back of the machine which will remove only this one disc from the system. Everything else will continue to run as it is right now."

"Okay then. Do your thing." The manager disappeared into a back room where the main console was located.

Mary placed her tool bag on the floor in the back of the troubled machine. She removed a tool from the bag and used it to open the back of the machine. She knew the location of the off-line switch, but even had she not, it was clearly marked above the toggle switch: OFF LINE. She flipped the switch.

The room went quiet. *Oh my God*, she thought. It was as though power was lost to the building. Everything stopped working.

The manager ran into the room from the back, yelling "What did you do?"

"I just flipped the switch to take the disc off line, but everything went down."

"You crashed the entire system."

"I'm so sorry. That wasn't supposed to happen."

"I tried to turn the system back on, but it won't come back on. I've got retailers going crazy."

"Okay, okay. I'm going to flip the switch and put this disc back into the system the way it is. Try to bring it back on line now."

She returned the toggle switch to its original position. The manager ran back to the console room. Mary heard the equipment start up again. She breathed a small sigh of relief. At least the system was back up. The manager returned.

"I don't want that to happen again."

"Neither do I. I'm going to leave this machine alone and inform my dispatch of what happened. IBC will send someone who specializes on this piece of equipment. I'm so sorry." She packed her tool bag and left the premises.

When Mary arrived at work on Monday, she was directed to return to Richard's Bank. IBC had sent design engineers from Florida to troubleshoot the disc and they wanted her input.

When she arrived at the bank there were three IBC engineers in pastel colored, light weight suits standing in front of the troubled machine. There were also two computer managers standing around. Mary overheard the conversation as she approached.

"She must have done something wrong. The machine won't take down the system if you just switch it off line."

"Yeah," another engineer chimed in. "I took a look at the switch and it's fine. The circuit is connected just as it should be."

Mary approached the group, "Good morning."

The first engineer spoke up, "Hi, you're the tech who responded to the call over the weekend?"

"I am."

"What did you do?"

"I flipped the switch marked off line and the system crashed."

"No, that can't be."

"That's what I said, and I've taken discs off line before so it was a shock when the system crashed, but that's what happened."

"Okay, well you can wait in the office with Mark. We'll take care of it now."

"That works for me." Mary opened the door to the office where Mark worked. Because it was a major account, the bank had been assigned a fulltime on-site IBC engineer with his own office, which opened into the computer room.

"Hey Mark, the design engineers dismissed me and sent me in here to help you."

"Hi Mary. I heard you had a difficult time this weekend."

"Yes, I felt really bad when the system crashed. All I can say is that it never happened like that before."

"Yeah, the engineers have been saying that it couldn't crash just by taking it off line. They're blaming it all on you."

"Well, when they move to take it off line it'll be back on them."

The two coworkers laughed at the expense of the engineers.

"What can I help you with Mark?"

"I heard you've become an expert at cleaning printer cartridges."

"Yeah, I saw Larry take one apart, clean all the pieces then put it back together, but I didn't realize that the letters have to go back in a certain order. So when I cleaned one of the printers at the demonstration center, the print came out garbled and Bob helped me figure out how to get the letters back in the correct order. It was funny."

"Yeah, I heard, but it's amazing that you were able to put it back together after seeing it done only once."

"Really? I just watched how Larry put it back together, taking it apart was easy. But, like I said, I didn't realize he was putting the letters back in any particular order."

"Well, I have two printers out there that could use a good cleaning; the printouts are getting hard to read."

"Sure, I'll do that for you."

"Okay, well you sit here--" Mark indicated she should sit at his desk, "and I'll take one of the printers off line and bring the cartridge to you."

"Be careful not to crash the system."

They laughed.

Mary was sitting alone at Mark's desk, dismantling a printer cartridge when she heard the computer room go quiet. She opened the door to Mark's office, but did not venture into the computer room. There was mayhem. One of the computer managers was screaming.

"You said it wouldn't crash the system! You kept blaming the female, but she told you what would happen and you did it anyway!"

"Sir, I'm sorry. We'll bring the system back up immediately."

Mark approached his office and smiled at Mary. The two reentered the office and closed the door.

"Well, Mary, it looks like you've been vindicated."

"Yeah, but I feel sorry for those poor engineers. If they hadn't been trying so hard to blame me, they might have thought to physically remove the machine from the system if indeed it did go down. Between the three of them it wouldn't have taken longer than a minute if they had prepared for it."

"I don't feel sorry for them; they've been blaming you since they first got here."

Mary finished cleaning the printer cartridges for Mark, then departed to return to headquarters. The Florida engineers had arranged to return at midnight to take down the entire system then repair the disc. Mark had stated, "Heck, we could have done that," causing Mary to laugh yet again.

Back at headquarters, no one spoke of the situation at Richard's. Mary knew that had she messed up it would be all they wanted to talk about. She scoured at the pettiness of her coworkers.

After two years at IBC she hated the thought of going to work. Mary's issues with time management were still a part of her life. She had been called on the carpet for failing to timely submit her incident reports, as well as for late arrivals to an account's 7:30 am scheduled maintenance appointment.

Mary ran into a fellow IBC employee from the New Jersey office. They had attended the basics class together in New York City. He was there to take a class in the DC office. When he asked how she was doing she told him that she was thinking about quitting. She had determined that the toll was not worth the reward, which could only be measured monetarily.

"Well, why would you quit?"

"What do you mean?"

"Remember, they taught us that if anyone inquires about our employment they only provide the date we started and the date we ended."

"Yeah, I guess I never really thought about what that meant."

"It means you may as well let them fire you and collect the severance check on the way out the door."

"Humph, it's something to think about."

"What will you do if you leave?"

"I'll make use of the G.I. bill and go to school. I've always wanted to own my own business."

'That's a lofty goal. Good luck to you."

"Thanks."

Mary's mind was churning. She reviewed the last meeting she had with the DC Manager.

"Mary, I'm told you received an outside telephone call at one of the client's locations from someone who wanted to offer you a job."

She thought about the telephone call which had occurred the day before. She had been accompanied by two of her coworkers from the headquarters department as she responded to a request to repair a console. She had not been trained on that piece of equipment and had to bring along assistance. So immediately she knew that one or both of the two men had reported back – not to her immediate manager, but to the DC Manager – dogs. She was so tired of people smiling in her face while looking for a nice soft spot to stab her in the back.

"Yes, I did."

"Who was it?"

"I don't know."

"How did they get the number to the customer's computer room?"

"I have no idea. I was shocked by the phone call. I don't even know if it was real."

"What do you mean? Why wouldn't it be real?"

"Because how would an outsider get the phone number to a customer's computer room?" She thought, *Hey! Look at that; I can Tango.*

"Did you make an appointment to meet them?"

"Yes, but that doesn't mean that I have to keep the appointment."

"Mary, frankly it would be unfair for IBC to spend so much money training you, and then you run off to another company."

She thought, *You need to make up your mind, either you want me here or you don't.* She said, "Because someone offers me another job doesn't mean that I have to accept it."

"Well, I also wanted to discuss your timeliness. Even though your start time is 9:00 am, you have an account with a scheduled maintenance which begins at 7:30 am. Mary, you have to be there on time. They have allotted that specific time for maintenance in order to reduce the impact of losing their system availability; 7:40 or 7:45 is not acceptable."

"I've been trying; early morning is difficult for me. There is also a problem with parking in that area. There are very few parking lots in that area and they are allocated to monthly contracts only. Street parking is unavailable that early in the morning because of rush hour traffic. I have to first find a place to park five or six blocks away then walk back."

"You have to solve those issues, get started earlier if you need to."

"Well, have you thought about assigning that account to one of the early starters? I would be willing to exchange with someone who doesn't want a late evening maintenance schedule."

"No. This is your account and you have to fulfill the maintenance schedule."

"I'll do my best." She said it without resolve. It was just to end the fruitless conversation. She knew she was going to be late to that account again and so did he.

It was Sunday afternoon, the next morning she was due to perform scheduled maintenance at 7:30 am.

Mary thought, *Do I give up the battle? I am not a quitter, but I am so tired of fighting against the entire system and two-faced people who smile in my face as they plan their next backstabbing move. Two years is long enough to allow for acceptance; if it hasn't occurred by now it isn't going to happen; but I love what I do and it's too bad I have to give it up.*

There, with startling precision she realized that she had made a decision. She walked into her bedroom and set her alarm clock for 8:00 am.

The next morning she walked into the DC Manager's office, carrying her tool bag. She had been summoned but she knew what was waiting. She sat quietly and endured the speech, while an unidentified man in a suit stood in the corner to observe.

After the manager had gone through the reasons why he *had* to release her, he actually stated, "Mary? Is there anything you want to say that could help me avoid this action?"

"No."

He pulled the center desk drawer towards him and reached in to pick up an envelope.

"Here is your final check. It includes a severance amount."

Mary stood and reached to accept the envelope. "Thank you. I'm leaving my tool bag here with you." She turned and left his office, left the administrative offices, left the building.

The feeling of failure was not a good one, even though she did not think the failure was necessarily hers. She knew that no matter how much she did it was never going to be enough for shortsighted people.

She was off on a new adventure; she was going to college to learn to operate her own business.

Two days later she received a telephone call at home. It was the same caller as had reached her at the customer's computer center. He introduced himself as Dave and then asked her to come in for an interview. She informed him that she was looking forward to enrolling in college, and was not certain whether she wanted to be available for a full-time position.

"Well, why don't you come in and we can discuss it. If you decide not to accept, you won't have lost anything."

"That's true. Sure, I'll come in."

"Can you come in at 11:00 am tomorrow morning?"

"Yes, I can."

"Good, here's the address ...."

"Okay, I'll see you tomorrow at 11:00."

"Great. I'm looking forward to meeting you. Good-bye."

"Good-bye."

As Mary entered the building she walked over a giant seal which had been inset into the marble floor. She noted it was there, but did not pay attention to it. She waited at the reception desk for Dave who arrived with another male in tow.

Introductions were made all around then Dave and Jeff lead Mary to the elevators. "Dave and Jeff" – something made Mary wonder if those were their true names. They exited the elevator then approached a door with a security keypad. Dave gained access and they entered through the door into a computer room.

She was guided to a room in the back. The room was approximately twenty feet wide by fourteen feet deep. It was set up as an office with a tool clad workbench extended across the fourteen foot wall to the left. Mary eyed the workbench with envy. It contained all the tools she had become accustomed to while working at IBC, plus.

"Wow!," she had mistakenly spoken aloud.

Dave did the talking. "Yeah, it's a nice work station isn't it?"

"It surely is."

"Mary, we want you to accept the position as the on-site tech. This would be your office."

"Really, would I have sole responsibility for the entire room? What if I couldn't fix something."

"This is all IBC equipment and we have a contract with them if you find you need assistance."

The irony was not lost on Mary. She smiled at the two men, invoking smiles in return. They all recognized the irony.

"You guys know that I just left IBC, right?"

"We do."

"Humph."

"If you decide to take the job you'll work a regular eight hour workday and if something goes wrong at night, you'll be called first. So you get to decide whether to take the overtime or call IBC."

"This is sounding great."

"Would you like to fill out an application?"

"Sure."

Dave pulled open a desk drawer and removed an application. It had obviously been placed there beforehand. He handed the application to Mary.

As Mary accepted the application, she froze. Written across the top in big, bold letters were the words: CENTRAL INTELLIGENCE AGENCY. She involuntarily released a low level grunt.

"What's wrong?"

"Does this mean that I would be a direct employee of the CIA?"

"Yes, but our pay scale is comparable to the private sector."

"I appreciate that but it's not the salary that I'm concerned about."

"Talk to me, what's the issue?"

"I think my top secret security clearance is still in effect, but doesn't the CIA periodically inquire into employees' personal lives?" She was remembering the response provided by her mother when the FBI agents had conducted the initial investigation. The neighbors had similar responses. The FBI had caused quite a stir and was the cause of much speculation into Mary's supposed activities. One resulting rumor actually assigned her the dubious title of mistress to a Mafia kingpin. People allowed their imaginations to run away with them.

She did not look forward to having to dispel any such future rumors. It had been difficult enough the first time and she was not certain that she had managed to clarify the issue with everyone. Plus, she had been uncomfortable when the neighbors had actually ventured to ask questions about the type of equipment she was trained to repair. She had only responded, "The top secret kind."

"Yes, we have annual security reviews, but you won't have to do anything, they're automatic."

"That's the problem. I don't want the government probing around in my private life or creating interest in my life for people that I only say hello and good-bye to." She glanced over at the equipment in the computer room and imagined the type of information contained on those computers. "Additionally, if there were a leak out of the CIA, I would be first suspect. This is definitely one job that is too good to be true."

"I'm sorry you feel that way."

Jeff finally spoke up, "Why don't you take the application with you. I'll put my phone number here at the top and if you change your mind just give me a call."

"Thank you, I'll consider it."

As she was headed out she took a look at the flooring, finally noting the inset seal which exclaimed "Central Intelligence Agency."

She thought, *I must learn to pay attention to my surroundings.* Then an unanswerable question popped into her mind. *Did the CIA have something to do with me leaving IBC.*

Mary stepped from the building into the bright sunlight of a beautiful June day in Washington, DC. *That's it*, she thought, *I'm done allowing people to manipulate me. I'm going to college then I'll become a successful business owner; and my business will treat people fairly and actually reward them for the work they perform.*

Life Mark:
Spiritual Development

The prior chapters have taken you from pre-birth to age 23, the period during which my basic personality was formed. Following my two year stint at IBC, I went on to study for two years at a Junior College and never looked back. Beyond that period there are two major events which led me to a new outlook upon life. I would like to share those two events with you.

Considering the many times I was attacked by evil I can only say that I must have been wearing blinders not to have recognized that I was a target for evil. That recognition came late in my life. Upon receiving that revelation I developed an appreciation for an early connection with God. For so long I delayed the search for God, mainly because I did not want to accept my sins or cease my favorite sinful behaviors. I was defiant.

For so many years I did not recognize the Bible as the guide to life that it is. I was simply proceeding through life with no directive and labeling the things that happened to me as "life," not recognizing that a relationship with God held the key to a better life.

When I did take the time to listen to a preacher, I did not extract the innovation of the Bible being a guide to life. I viewed the Bible as a

"Book of Yoke." I knew it as a directive of *Don'ts*, never paying attention to the *Dos*.

My earliest efforts to build a relationship with God yielded preachers who were consumed by the need to warn of damnation. I quickly tired of hearing what I had *better not* do.

I am also nonresponsive to preachers who stress a wife's submission during every other Sunday service. Had they actually taught God's complete plan of family structure as defined in the Bible, instead of stressing that one directive for the wife, I might have been more receptive.

I can recall hearing only one male spiritual leader truly teach of each family member's responsibilities to God and family, including the husband.

Could it be that many of our male spiritual leaders extract that "submission" passage because it is self-serving? Surprise, surprise. Well, husband of mine, if you do as you are directed, then I will have no need to step around your lead.

During the majority of my young adult years, I ventured into a church here and there, every now and then. I would attend services prepared for a great revelation in my life, but it was not to be found in any of the churches I entered, or perhaps I was not truly ready to hear the Word. I was beginning to think that I might never have a church home, until I "truly" went in search of the right church home for my sons.

In 1983, while working in downtown D.C., I befriended a coworker who was excited about her relationship with God. We spoke often and I decided to find a church home for my sons and myself. I did not want to attend the same church as my friend because hers was a very large church. I wanted to be a part of a more personalized group of worshipers. I wanted to get to know the other church members and become like family, a church family.

Every Sunday for six weeks I walked or rode the bus to a different church with my then three and six year old sons in tow. The first five weeks were marked with screaming or sleep inducing preachers who delivered confusing messages that rang untrue to my heart. I wanted my sons to learn of God's grace and I wanted the messages to be clear and concise.

On the 6th Sunday, the children and I entered the doors of James' Memorial Church of Christ in southeast. As I walked through the church's entry foyer into the sanctuary I felt a slight tremble enter through the top of my head and travel downward through my body. I interpreted that tremble as a sign that I was in the right church.

Bishop Ashton Helms delivered an upbeat sermon extolling the benefits of being one of God's children. I had found our church home.

I had to get used to my pastor's method of doing things. I noticed that he had a habit of calling out people about their unGodly behaviors from the pulpit. I did not think he should do that in the presence of the entire congregation. I sometimes have to force myself to remember that God's ministers remain human, susceptible to the same shortfalls as the rest of us.

He was not perfect, but he was a good teacher and a great leader.

I liked that Bishop Helms taught not only by use of his sermons, but by example also. He and his wife, Madge, invited my sons and me to their home on several occasions. They were very kind to us. Madge gingerly guided me through the political aspects of the church so that I would not become ensnared in veiled conflicts.

My husband even decided to join us on some Sundays. Shortly thereafter I learned that an unsaved spouse has a path to God through his or her saved spouse.

Finally, my family was connected to God as we proceeded into the future with spiritual guidance. Evil did not want to accept it.

Four years after I joined the church under Bishop Helms' leadership, I received a telephone call at home on a Saturday afternoon. I recognized the voice of Deacon James as he asked, "Miss Mary, are you sitting down?"

"*Uh-oh*," I thought. I took a seat. "I am now Deacon James."

"Bishop Helms died of a heart attack earlier today. He was in his minivan on the 495 beltway.

He managed to stop the van and bring it to a complete halt so no one else was harmed, but he's gone."

"Oh, my God," the words were sluggish as they barely escaped my lips.

My spiritual leader was gone. Madge lost her husband. I grabbed up the children and drove to their home. When I arrived, there was barely room to park. I entered the home and quickly found Madge. She was hiding out in a back bedroom. I expressed my sorrow and offered my assistance with anything she needed.

I asked if she needed to get away, but she was concerned for the mourning family members and church members. She realized that her presence brought comfort to them. True Christians think beyond themselves. It was a deficiency that I had to work on (I have improved but I am still working on it).

Yes, my spiritual leader was gone, but evil could not erase his teachings. I had already stepped into the light. Again, evil failed to claim my soul.

✌ · | · ✌

In early 2011, I attended services at a church in Cheraw, South Carolina. I had driven past it and many other churches for five years, but for some reason that particular church held a special draw. At the end of the pastor's sermon he asked if anyone in the church wanted to receive the gift of speaking in tongues. My hand could not go up fast enough.

I knew that the gift of tongues is actually the voice of the Holy Spirit and I definitely wanted to experience the Holy Spirit speaking through me. (By the way, the person speaking in tongues does not usually have the ability to understand the words spoken by the Holy Spirit. I have been told there is a separate gift of interpretation. One person may speak in tongues while another may be able to "interpret." Recently I learned that when one speaks in tongues, the Holy Spirit within is praying directly to God.)

The pastor assigned a husband and wife team to accompany me to a room behind the sanctuary. The couple instructed me to simply open my mouth and allow the Holy Spirit to speak. As they prayed over me they began to speak in tongues. I heard audible syllables that were not arranged in the normal structure of the English language, nor any other language that my ear could identify.

However, when I opened my mouth what came from my vocal cords sounded more like yelps, quips and cries. I felt a power racking my body internally. It felt as though the Holy Spirit was in anguish. As the tears rolled down my face, the yelps and cries grew louder. My ears could not comprehend but my body detected a state of despair which I assumed to be because of the current status of God's people. The couple allowed the "speaking" for approximately ten minutes before they closed out the session.

I was elated that I had actually felt the Holy Spirit inside my body, even though the vocalizations which rolled across my tongue were not the same as those coming from the couple. I was also frightened by the fact that the Holy Spirit was in such anguish. I began to ask myself, *What can I do with my life to make things better?*

As I drove home from the church the Holy Spirit began speaking again. I forced myself to concentrate on the road instead. I was afraid I might cause an accident.

When I arrived at home I allowed my mind to proceed in its normal fashion. I was alone. I began preparing dinner. The Holy Spirit began speaking through me at will; I felt the same anguish and despair. It would speak in spells of five to ten minutes then allow my body to rest.

Physically, it felt as though my internal organs were bruised. I did not mind. I already knew the Holy Spirit to be powerful; I had not expected, however, to actually feel the power. It made me feel special even though I know that this experience is available to everyone.

The Holy Spirit continued to speak through me at random intervals over the next two weeks or so. I could not control when it began to speak, though I could stop the process, usually when I was driving or when I needed to take a break from the power that racked me internally. It was truly an unforgettable experience; one which I revisit often.

Aftermath:
A Self Analysis

This epilogue is an evaluation of who I am and why I have become the person I am. I have no formal training in psychology or social work, nor have I sought any consultations or help of any kind from psychologists, psychiatrists, books or any other source which attempts to analyze the process of the human mind. What follows is truly a *self-* analysis.

Damaged though my soul may be, by the grace of God it still belongs to me. Evil has not taken possession of my soul. I do not profess to be an angel by any stretch of the imagination, but I am a good person. The medical community makes use of a motto which I have adopted as a guide for life: *First do no harm.*

In reflection I find it easy to identify evil, but while in the midst of the events brought about by the hand of evil it is simply a matter of dealing with the immediate situation. There is often not enough time to dwell on why. Additionally, lessons learned have revealed that there are often hidden parties at work – parties who may manage never to be unveiled. Only with innocent intent can the quest to find a solution to a problem be accomplished with soul intact.

I seek merely to solve the present issue, whatever that may be then prepare in wait for the next issue, which undoubtedly lurks around the next corner. Reluctantly, I admit that it is sometimes difficult to let go of animosities for those who would deliberately orchestrate troubles in my life. Often I have thoughts of revenge, but when I suffer that sin of thought I ask myself if those people are worth the loss of my soul. The answer is and must always be, "No!"

I have come to realize that my life impacts the lives of others; definitely those who are close to me and sometimes people who are incidental, by mere close proximity or even by accident. I wish to always provide a positive impact.

The Early Days

Starting at the beginning, my memory of pre-existence is a true memory which has been strong since early childhood. That memory confirms for me the existence of life beyond human consciousness. It also causes me to question whether I have lived a prior existence, but I have no memory to support that prospect.

I have, of course, no memory of the events surrounding my birth; I have compiled the conversation based on the few facts relayed by my mother. It was difficult for my siblings and me to get information from my mother. Thus, when she was in a reminiscing mood we were all ears.

At birth, the doctor chose to clip the end of my tongue, informing my parents that it was best for me. I have no way of knowing whether the doctor understood the devastation his action would cause in my life and had deliberately allowed the hand of evil to use his position as a trusted professional or whether he truly thought he was doing what was best for me, and so, in the absence of that knowledge, I make no accusations.

Nonetheless, having ugly, flared teeth was a dominant issue and a continuous foundation for discontent in my life. In this country an easier, if not better, life is afforded those with money and/or beauty. To have neither is to constantly face an uphill climb.

Yet, aside from society's tendency to overlook me, my own sense of self-worth often suffered under the weight of the knowledge that I would never achieve the societal "A" list.

I was not often in a state of downward spiral, but the injustice of it would hit me in infrequent spells. I might have been able to accept being a "Plain Jane" a bit easier, but having an obvious malformation actually stunted my social development and left me with an intermittent inferiority complex.

Because I perceive myself as having been ostracized by the mainstream I definitely possess a tender soul. An ill-placed comment could leave me in search of either solitude or a biting retort. I have developed a desire for solitude, for it is the only time I do not feel the judgment of others, which I admit may sometimes be incorrectly perceived.

Evil attacked most egregiously during the events of my baby sister's death. The events as relayed are from the memory of a preschooler. I attempted to obtain a copy of the file from the records branch of the Metropolitan Police Department in Washington, DC, but my efforts were unsuccessful. I expected that because I am a victim and a relative of another victim that there would be no issue. Instead I learned that the Police Department guards the case files as though they were made of gold. Even a second attempt through the Department's FOIA Office (Freedom of Information Act) proved fruitless.

I learned from a family member that the woman who was supposed to be providing care for my brother, sister and me received a jail sentence. Still, I have so many questions. I want to know the name of the woman who was the supposed caregiver; for that matter I also want to know the identities of the boys. Were they her children or were they additional children for whom she was supposed to be providing care? Did the supposed caregiver orchestrate the events of that day? Did she return to the crime scene? How much jail time did she receive and where was she housed? Where is she now and does she have regrets over the events of that day? Did she and my mother have a prior relationship?

Bella Annette was a sweet, playful baby and I felt the loss of my little sister. I recall being unable to sleep. My young mind was too uninformed to connect the dots. No one would talk to me about it.

I was told that Bella was dead but no one explained what death meant. I have no memory of my sister's actual funeral service, but I have a vivid memory of her interment service. I could not understand why they placed my baby sister in a box then lowered that box into the ground. I was horrified by what *they* were doing to her.

At such an early age I realized just how fleeting life can be. Aside from the loss of my sister, the events of that day left me leery of people in general. I do not make friends easily. People are often drawn to me but I am not very receptive. There are a handful of people whom I list in the friendship column, but Alissa remains my one true friend with whom I share every aspect of my life. Still, there are events in this book which will be news to her, such as the attempted rape and the threat against my life.

I think also, that I moved beyond the day of my sister's death with an unhealthy distrust of authority figures. Following Bella's death, my mother, her boyfriend, police officers and health care workers were all involved in ascertaining the events. My brother and I were questioned over and over about what happened. I remember wondering whether anyone believed me.

Also, I remember everyone asking me to describe the boys. It made me believe that the three boys were not supposed to be there, or perhaps the babysitter denied their existence. In addition to the interrogations, I underwent a very degrading and improperly conducted intimate examination.

As a result of the many interrogations, I determined that authority figures were unable to provide answers or solutions. They were only good at providing questions.

Everyone ignored the needs of the two surviving children. It would have been a good time to explain the existence of God. I believe I would have felt comforted to know that my sister was with God. It certainly comforts me now, but my only outlet then was to place the events of Bella's last day into the dark recesses of my mind. In order to move forward I had to erase the unanswerable.

With the erasure of Bella's death from my mind I set a precedent for erasure of all the hurtful parts of my life. That ability was too handy. Instead of analyzing and creating learning elements as guides for my life, I would throw away the facts and restart life anew. I never realized just how dangerous the habit could be. It became a survival technique, pure and simple.

The Mother/Daughter Relationship

I have always admired my mother and sought to be a strong independent woman, just like her. Any disapproval from her would cut through me like a knife. I often felt that there was no way I could please her. Even as I cared for her during the last six years of her life I felt her resentment at being dependent upon me.

I can only imagine the strains on my mother as she reared three children without assistance from the men who helped create them. My siblings and I were strong willed from early ages. We were not an easy bunch to control.

It was because of my mother that I developed a desire for independence and control. As my mother gained more and more independence, so I craved it as well. I experienced along with her the failed attempts at relationships and the resulting disappointments. I saw that she not only needed companionship, but an additional income could have helped to create the financial stability that was so desperately needed. I think I developed an underlying fear of marriage because I did not know how to maintain a relationship. I became determined to do it all on my own; I did not heed the well-known warning: *No man is an island.*

I think my desire for independence and control stems too from the fractured relationship between my mother and me. I never understood why my mother and I were unable to communicate on an academic level; every attempt ended sadly. Our relationship never grew beyond the level of parental directives.

My personal quest for independence did not aid in the goal to tighten the relationship with my mother. What I viewed as stepping out into the world to claim my little piece of it, I believe she viewed as me trying to get away from her.

That was far from the truth. In actuality, I returned to Washington, DC from Cherry Point, North Carolina because that was where my mother made her home. Had I been able to talk her into returning to South Carolina with me, I would have made my home there since 1973.

Our fractured relationship may also have had something to do with the beatings received during childhood and adolescence. The beatings generated hatred that dissipated in short order, but left behind emotional scars that would never heal.

I consider the absence of my father in my life to have caused a detriment in my ability to relate to men on a close and personal level, but, surprisingly, I do not ascribe any detrimental attributes to him directly.

The Truth About Corporal Punishment

As a recipient of corporal punishment I tend not to dwell on the beatings, but the fact that I survived them. I say to myself that it was not that bad, but the truth is that I retain vivid memories of those times when I thought the beatings were particularly vicious. Often I cannot remember the reasons for the beatings, but I remember asking myself why my mother hated me and why I was receiving beatings for lesser offenses than my sister or brother had committed?

Perhaps my offenses were not lesser than those of my siblings but I certainly thought so, therefore, the impression of inequality was great. Often, my mother would say "You should know better because you're the oldest." I thought to myself, *Knowledge isn't automatic, particularly not because you happen to be the first born*, but I dared not say it aloud.

Corporal punishment has unintended consequences. I am absolutely certain that my mother did not intend to mold me into an insecure adult who is afraid of success. Indeed, that was an unintended consequence. I believe the consequences relate to the characteristics of the individual receiving the beatings. In some instances the application of corporal punishment may mold a criminal or a drug/alcohol abuser. In my case the mold created an insecure lone wolf.

I often receive compliments regarding my skills and intelligence, yet I deliberately sidestep opportunities for greatness and question myself. Also, I have an internal self-destruct button which sometimes acts on its own accord to sabotage an opportunity. I can feel it about to happen, but I am powerless to prevent it, even when the only effort required is for me to stop talking.

The "insecure" characteristic is interpreted by users as a "person of prey." Twice I have actually attracted people who tried to convince me to use my body to enrich their personal finances; one of them was a woman. Luckily, I have a great sense of moral outrage which switches my mode from "prey" to definitive "lone wolf."

I manage to permanently separate myself from people who want to use me. I can be dangerous when in "lone wolf" mode. I will escape the danger at all costs. I am capable of physically harming someone I perceive as dangerous, as evidenced by the day I attacked my mother's boyfriend with a hammer. God's grace has prevented me from having to use that capability a second time. I have managed to remove myself from relationships that could take me down a dangerous path.

Although I began my foray into parenthood by applying corporal punishment, eventually the recognition arrived that it was cruel. Additionally, it was not providing the behavioral corrections I sought. At that point I announced to my sons that I would stop beating them. I began talking to them on an adult level about what I expected of them and why it would be to their benefit to adjust bad behaviors, such as lying. When punishments were necessary I began taking away their pleasure privileges, such as television, telephone, or time with their friends, usually for one or two weeks. The corrective results were better, though not always as great as I desired.

Incomplete Family Structure

During my early childhood I felt the absence of my father and grandparents. I instinctively knew that there was supposed to be someone in my life to let me know that I was loved during those times when I was not feeling the love from my mother. I knew that my mother loved me but I do not ever remember hearing her say it; a detriment. Since adolescence and well into my thirties I believed that my maternal grandmother was watching over me and assisting me from her position beyond the grave. I do not believe that I have completely released that belief because it helps me to think that I can feel the love of my grandmother, whom I never had the opportunity to meet. However, my faith is now so much stronger that I recognize God as the bearer of all my gifts and blessings.

I have come to believe in the extended family theory. Presently, I would find it difficult to live in a household of twenty to thirty people. Yet, doesn't it provide a better developmental environment for children when they grow up with grandparents, parents, aunts, uncles, sisters, brothers and cousins? The richest portion of my childhood develop occurred when we lived in my uncle's home with his family, while another uncle and his family lived next door. Surprisingly, I do not recall receiving beatings during that period.

I can remember one or the other of my uncles intervening on my and my brother's behalf. They would say, "Mae (they used my mother's middle name), leave those children alone. Why don't you let them play outside in the backyard?"

I loved spending time with my uncles and cousins, but after we were scattered throughout the city I rarely saw any of them.

It was not until my family and I lived in a housing project run by the government that I was made aware of the fact that my absentee father created a detriment outside of our household.

Others tagged us as secondary citizens because we were a single parent household. We breathed, slept and ate no differently than anyone else. Certainly the children could not be held responsible for the status of the parents' marriage, and yet, we *were* held responsible.

The Shock of Becoming An Adult

During both my military service and my time at IBC I felt the sting of unjust judgment. How could any intelligent person assign ability or intelligence by gender alone? Had I not been able to perform the tasks assigned to me that four-year period could merely be tagged a mistake. Yet, my performance was well above average and my expulsion can only be assigned to meritless prejudices and preconceived notions.

In the case of my relationship with Jaime, I accept a certain amount of responsibility and attribute some of the disastrous conclusion to our relationship to my own inexperience; although no one can ever be excused from attempting or threatening to kill another human being. During the course of that relationship I was simply enjoying the relationship day by day and had not bothered to look ahead or to consider what he might have expected from the relationship.

I realized at the time that I was unwilling to give up my newfound freedom and independence. However, having made a true assessment of my feelings after so many years have passed, I also realize that while I was willing to allow a man to have total control over when and how we spent our time together, I was definitely not willing to allow him to have control over my entire life. I was frightened when I learned on that last night that my future had been planned without a single inquiry into what I wanted out of life, not even where I wanted to live. The conveyance of our future together had made no mention of my career.

Instantly I saw all of *my* plans dissipate into a cloud of smoke and reappear as a picture of a woman standing at a kitchen stove, barefoot and pregnant and surrounded by a loud swarm of hungry little children, pleading for their dinner. That woman was faceless, it was not me. I have never been able to picture myself as a traditional housewife.

Additionally, I have always wondered whether the outcome of that night and my actions on the following day kept me from being listed among the throng of battered wives. Perhaps it was a narrow escape.

I can never allow anyone to have total control over my life. To be perfectly honest, it is one of the issues which has slowed the development of my relationship with God. I have difficulty letting go, which one must do in order to let God.

The issue of relinquishing control may also have contributed to my decision to wage battle against the authority of my commander at Electronics School. As

I take a look at his actions, I cannot hold any animosity toward him. I find that while he personally treated me with contempt, he was also mindful of my career and was very careful to do as little damage to it as he could get away with. The pro and con marks he assigned during the office hours were not designed to be destructive.

Amid our battle I developed a healthy respect for him, though I was very careful not to allow him to see it. It did not dawn on me until the construction of this book that my incessant refusal to honor that one command decision might have damaged his career. That was never my intention; I hope that he has been able to forgive the crazy bravery of an American teenager.

I believe it to be my experience at IBC that has caused me to develop a cynical and responsive nature. I faced such an uphill battle at IBC that it seemed every time I got within reach of the top of the mountain, the mountain grew taller. In my search for allies, I thought there might be at least one female on board. Instead, the women were more openly contemptuous than the men. It felt as though they were outraged that I would dare attempt to operate in what they deemed to be the world of men. They, too, wanted to control my life. (So many people want to run my life for me. I have found this to be a recurring issue in my life – one which I continue to battle against.)

To the women who want to define womanhood within the limitations of a small box I say, "Do not attempt to define me by the miniscule boundaries you have set for yourself." Not only do I have a feminine nature but I also have a proficiency for things electrical and mechanical.

Not only have I delivered children, am a great cook, can crochet, knit, make clothing and window curtains, but I have also designed and remodeled a kitchen, designed and built a kitchen from the floor up, installed plumbing and a garbage disposal, laid hardwood, tile and ceramic flooring, installed sinks and toilets, repaired walls, stripped brick from a wall, installed lighting and cut a countertop in order to make a refrigerator fit an undersized space. If you prefer to ask a man to do these things for you that is fine, but please do not ascribe your fears to me.

I am unable to understand why some people ascribe preconceived notions or dare to define boundaries for others. Because of this lack of understanding I have become what I call a "Reactionist."

If someone offers me sugar, I will respond with sugar. My spirit is always receptive. I can even be generous. Some say I can be generous to a fault, but I do not believe that to be possible. It is, however, possible to be generous to the wrong person.

On the other hand, if someone treats me with contempt I can be equally contemptuous. I have left a few people wishing they had never met me. The "Reactionist" theory is similar to "an eye for an eye," but not quite as exact.

As the memory of the coworker who placed me in the middle of his marriage returned to me, I felt outrage. He must have anticipated that I would be reluctant to spend my time with a married man and, therefore, he hid vital information from me. His actions were just as offensive as those of my would be rapist when I was ten years old. Both men took advantage of my innocence. Eventually I was able to let go of the animosities I held toward both men; but luckily, when we forgive another it is not required that we re-associate with that person.

I attribute my need for change to not being truly accepted into my field. I have spent my life collecting stuff, like most everyone else, I suspect. However, unlike most everyone else, I do not mind letting go of my stuff. I actually think to myself that I will replace it with stuff that I like better. I get bored with anything monotonous, while change represents the opportunity for greater fulfillment. Change offers adventure and opportunity.

I need change; a continuous newness in my life. There are some factors that can remain constant, but there must be change happening around those constants or I begin to look about in search of something different. The something different could be something as small as a quick two-day course on picture framing, as large as remodeling a kitchen, or even as drastic as relocating four hundred miles away from everyone and everything with which I am familiar.

Happiness Can Be Found

That phase of my life which was dependent upon governmental assistance was degrading, just as it was deliberately designed to be. Still, I am proud to say that my hopes and desires for a bright future were and still are absolute. It is a point which declares me a winner. Evil did not get my soul.

It is true that money does not provide happiness; and, conversely, the lack of money does not prevent happiness.

I have been lucky enough that I have experienced financial stability within my life; however, that stability was always predicated on the next two paychecks. Like most Americans, I lived with the unadulterated knowledge that I was only two paychecks or one medical affliction away from abject poverty.

Even though money provides the solution to financial stability, it also comes attached with concerns for protecting, investing and preserving it. Worry over the preservation of money has caused some people to lose sleep and others to take their lives.

During the most recent explosion of the banking industry I listened to news reports in utter amazement as I learned of fathers who killed themselves, leaving their families in despair, simply because they lost access to money. I wonder if any of them considered that the loss of money might have been temporary or that the loss presented to their families upon their deaths was a greater loss than the money.

In some cases, fathers actually killed their entire families before killing themselves. Now, that was truly an act of insanity. To surrender the lives of your innocent loved ones because of money, or the lack of it, is truly to have lost your perspective. Worship of the almighty dollar is unwise; it is extremely detrimental to the worshiper and perhaps to his or her loved ones as well.

Even though I have memories of longing for more money than was currently in my possession, my happiest memories are of events which required minimal costs, if any at all, such as the smile brought to a child's face at a small birthday celebration when surrounded by family and friends, the joy brought by or to a friend with the purchase of an inexpensive greeting card or a well-timed telephone call when the receiving party needed to be lifted up.

Final Word

Damaged does not mean irreparable, nor broken, nor lost.

My life can hardly be described as the model of perfection. I have suffered many bumps and bruises. Yet, I have managed to maintain possession of my soul and I have come to realize that God has always been with me.

For years I asked the question, "Why am I here." Finally, I realized that the purpose of Jesus' life was to be an example for everyone else. Does not everyone have that same purpose?

Experience has taught me many lessons, the two most prevalent of which are (1) humor is one of God's saving graces; and (2) building with God is about enrichment, not riches.

I do not know whether I will ever be a perfect Christian, or even whether God expects it. However, I find contentment in the simple effort to reach that goal.

If your life is consistently wrought with havoc, ask yourself why. Examine every aspect of your life, particularly your earliest memories.

Recognize that unprovoked attacks most likely signal God's presence in your life, not His absence. The attacks are intended to guide you away from Him and His blessings. Don't be fooled; view your life from God's point of view.

About the Author

Mary Arnold is a retired legal secretary, the mother of two and grandmother of two. *Damaged Soul* is her initial foray into the publishing world.

Ms. Arnold currently resides in the place of her birth, Chesterfield County, South Carolina. She is grateful for the peace and quiet of rural South Carolina which affords the opportunity for her creative writing abilities to flourish.

Ms. Arnold was reared, educated and spent the majority of her employment history in the nation's Capital. Washington, D.C. will always hold a special place in her heart.

> From another plain
> My soul did rise
> With challenges behind
> It is clear to my eyes
>
> Damaged though
> My soul may be
> By the grace of God
> It still belongs to me
>
> Evil still battles
> Trying to win
> But my Father in heaven
> I *will* see again
>
> ~ Mary R. Arnold

About the Book Cover

In 2004 I boarded an airplane to travel across country. Blessed with a window seat and armed with a brand new digital camera, I decided to test my camera by taking scenery photographs through the window of the airplane.

Initially, I tried to capture air to ground scenery, but the clouds were not very cooperative. Then I began to capture photos of what I thought were some very interesting cloud formations.

The results were breathtaking, even when printed in black and white. Still, never would I have guessed that I would one day designate one of those photos as my book cover.

Two of those photos are on the following pages. Enjoy.

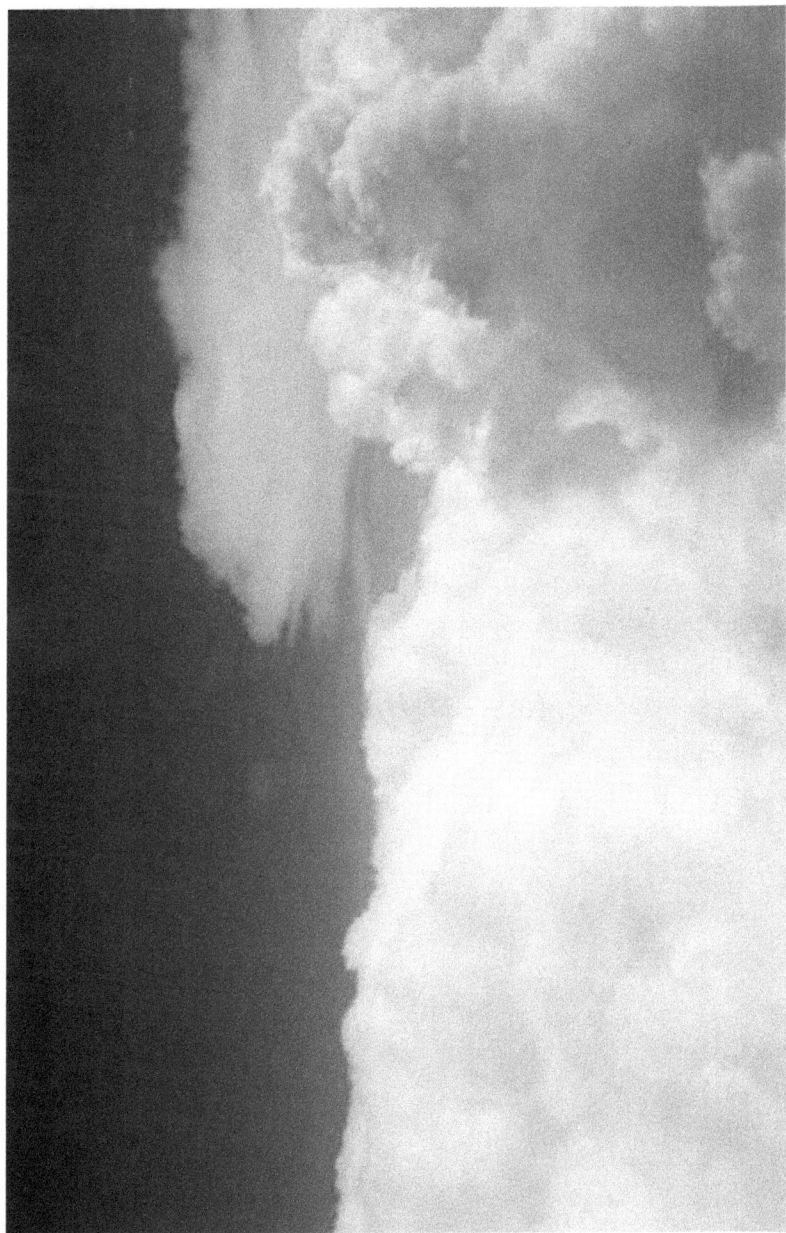

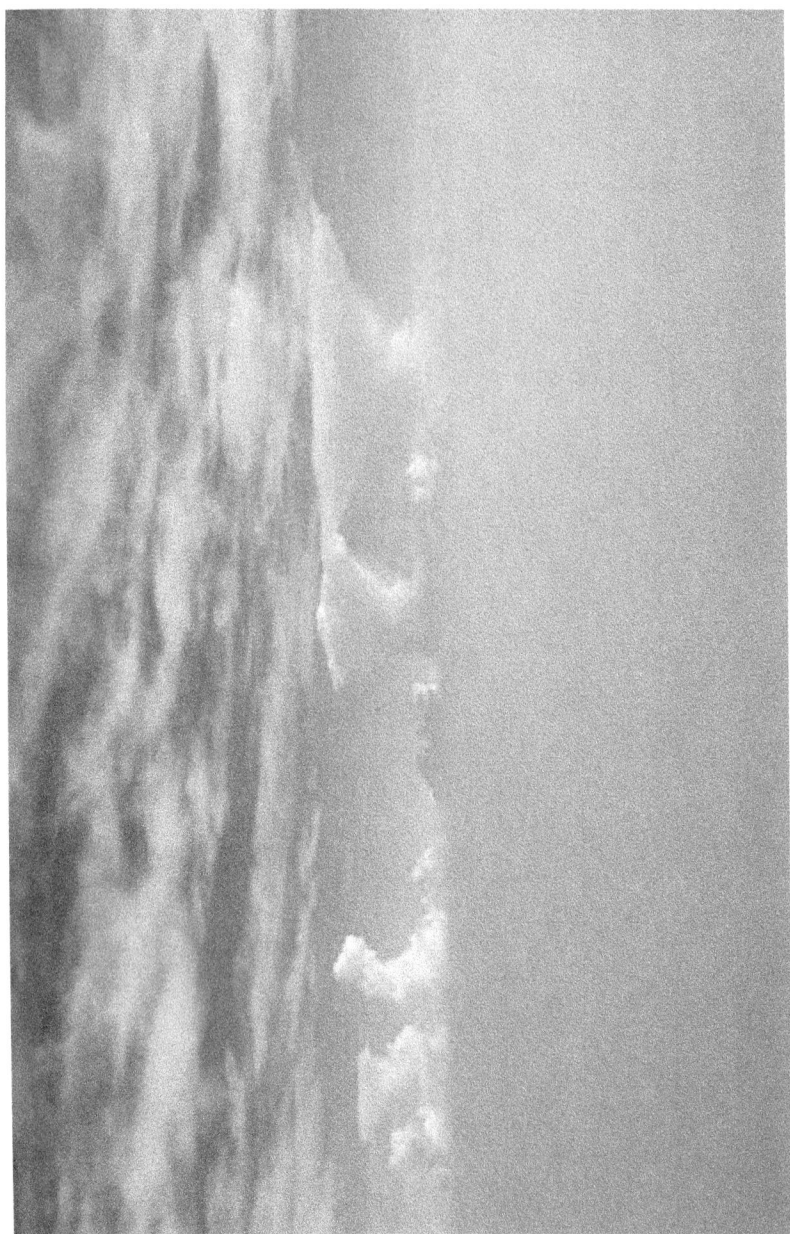

www.ingramcontent.com/pod-product-compliance
Lightning Source LLC
Chambersburg PA
CBHW052036090426
42739CB00010B/1932